The Complete Windows 10 Manual

(Updated for the new Spring Update)

Jason Miller

Table of Contents

Getting Started with Windows 10

The Windows desktop has gone through many changes in recent years, culminating in what you see on your monitor today. There's a lot of new content to look through, so read on to discover how to get up and running with Microsoft's latest version of Windows.

We even take a look at the new Spring Update, and what the future may hold for Windows 10.

Upgrading Keeping Windows Up-to-date

In the unlikely event that you are still running an older version of Windows, it is fairly easy to upgrade to Windows 10. Depending whether you are upgrading from Windows 7 or 8, or an older version such as Vista, the process is slightly different but not too difficult.

Upgrading from Windows 7 or 8

Installing Windows 10 on a Windows 7 or 8.1 PC is a relatively simple process, as long as you follow a few basic rules and ensure that the hardware specification matches with what is required by the newer operating system (OS).

The first thing you need to do is to make sure you have installed all of the updates for Windows 7 or Windows 8, including update KB3035583 so that you'll receive the "Get Windows 10" app. When you see the message pop-up, click the box and follow the instructions to begin installation.

Your PC will run through several things during this time, especially checking that everything installed and connected to it is OK with the update. You may be asked to identify whether the PC belongs to a company or if it's a personal PC, depending on the version of Windows being installed.

Next you'll be asked to sign in with your Microsoft account. If you have an Outlook.com, Hotmail or Xbox account you can use those details. If you don't have a Microsoft account, you can sign up for one. The final part of the account setup process is to choose a password or PIN login.

You will now see a series of screens explaining some of the new additions to Windows 10 and be given some choices as to file storage, new apps and how Cortana works. Windows 10 will now set up your new apps and load into the start-up screen. Log in to get going on the new OS.

Upgrading from Windows XP or Vista

You can't upgrade Windows to the new version directly from XP or Vista. Be sure to back up your files first or you will lose them.

1. Here we're doing a clean install from a USB drive copy of Windows 10. If you downloaded Windows you'll get some instructions on how to get it to this point. You can make a bootable windows USB using a variety of methods. There is a lo of helo available on Microsoft.com in now to make a bootable windows 10 USB. Once you have the bootable USB ready, you will need to force your BIOS to boot using the USB instead of the default hard disk, which contains your older version of windows. The way to change boot options in the BIOS will depend on your version of BIOS. If you are able to change the boot options to USB, you should see a similar screen on boot:-

2. Once you've pressed the key, the setup will start and you'll see the first screen. Click on "Install now" and you can see the next screen. This screen enables you to select the default language you want to install. Chances are you will also need to enter the product key for Windows at this stage. This will be included in your pack if you bought Windows 10 from a store or you'll have been given it if you downloaded Windows. If not sure, you can opt to enter the product key after installation.
3. Like all software, Windows 10 comes with a licence agreement that you'll need to accept. A necessary evil if you like. So tick the box and click Next. It gives you the authority to use the software and terms and conditions of use, and it's a legal agreement from Microsoft's side.
4. Then you will need to choose between custom installation and upgrade option. Since we are doint a fresh install, choose the custom option. It's likely that if you do. We're installing Windows only here, which is referred to as 'Custom'. You'll then be asked which drive you want to install Windows on.

5. When the actual installation process is completed, Windows 10 will begin the set up process detailed on the previous page, for Windows 7 or 8.1. You'll see several screens inviting you to set up your sign in details and various settings before you get to the new Windows 10 desktop.

Setting Up a Microsoft Account

A Microsoft account is an important part of using Windows 10. It gives you single sign in access to all of the Microsoft and Windows 10 services, from Skype and Office to Outlook and the Store. Setting one up should be the first thing you do in Windows 10

Set Up and Configure Your Account

Microsoft prefers its users to have a single main account. Here we show you how to create one as well as look at any other further settings you might need.

1. You can sign up for an account when you install or initialise Windows 10 for the first time but you can also create one at www.account.microsoft. com. This is also where you can customise your account settings, which we'll come onto shortly.

2. Even if you think you don't have a Microsoft account, it's quite possible that you do have one. Ever had a Hotmail or Outlook.com address, or did you use MSN or Windows Live Messenger? You can sign in with those same credentials.

3. In addition to Windows and Outlook.com, you can also use your account across all Microsoft services including Xbox Live, Skype, Office and Bing, as well as Windows-powered phones (your Contacts are automatically synchronised with your account too).

4. You can create a Microsoft account with any email address (you used to have to have an Outlook or Windows Live account). So even if you use Gmail, you can still get a Microsoft account. It's optional whether you have a new Outlook.com email account as well.

5. During the initialisation process for Windows 10, you will be asked to sign in using your Microsoft account (you can also sign in with a Local Account). Microsoft will then go and fetch any information connected to your account, such as your profile picture, etc.

6. Once you've signed in using your Microsoft account, you can configure it from within Windows 10. Open the main Settings and choose Accounts. You can change options to do with the account itself here as well as how often your computer should require you to sign in.

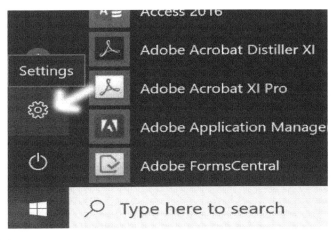

7. Clicking Manage your Account will take you to your account page online. You may see an update to your account terms and conditions when you do this for the first time. Here you can see recent purchases, your devices, personal info (plus payment info) and change your password.
8. Back in Settings > Accounts > Sync your Settings, you can tell your PC what details you want it to synchronise to your Microsoft account. Aside from several other options, you can choose whether you want your stored passwords to be synchronised using your account.
9. Services within Windows that use your Microsoft account, such as Mail or the Windows Store, will now automatically have your account details pre-filled. You will be able to get access to your purchase history and more via the individual apps.

10. Within Settings > Accounts you can also add family members to your PC, so they use their own login and don't have to share your account. You can specify time limits and restrict the type of games that can be played. You can even add people that aren't in your family group.

Setting Up Parental Controls

If you're sharing a Windows 10 computer with your children, or they have one for themselves, then setting them up with their own account can be helpful. A Windows 10 child account gives them freedom, whilst allowing you to set up certain restrictions.

Windows 10 Child Account

With a Windows 10 child account you're able to set up age restrictions and time limits and ensure they're not visiting sites or using apps they shouldn't.

1. There is an alternate way of getting to your account portal. Start off by clicking the Windows Start button and typing 'account'. The first result that should appear is Manage your account, if anything else appears, as in you have some work labelled 'account' or such, then scroll down until you find the Manage your account option.

2. You'll now find yourself at the Windows 10 Settings page, in the Accounts section portal. Notice there are links down the left-hand side, look for the Family & Other People link and click it to continue with the process.

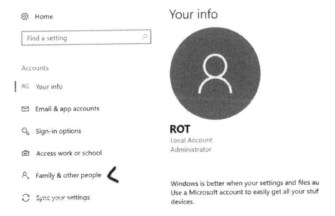

3. You'll need to sign in with a Microsoft account for this to work. If you've not already set up a main Microsoft login account for Windows, you'll need to click the Sign in with a Microsoft account option. Once done, you'll be presented with the current family members who already have MS accounts.

4. Next, click on the Add a Family Member link, by the plus sign under the Your Family section. This will launch a new pop-up window to create a new Microsoft account. You need to make sure that your child has an email address and that you or they can currently access it to authenticate the process.

5. Click the Add a Child option in the new account window and enter their email in the text box section below. When you're ready, click on the Next button.

6. You'll now get the message that it's not a Microsoft account, click the link to Create a Microsoft Account. This will bring you to a new window with the email address you've entered already filled in. Complete the relevant details and click the Next button to continue.

7. The next section details what level of search and advertising Microsoft will allow to the account. Obviously you can untick both boxes, or leave them as they are, depending on what you want. However, for the sake of enhanced privacy, we recommend unticking both. Click Next when you're ready.

8. The child's account is now ready to be activated. The message box informs you that you'll need to respond to the email Microsoft has sent before they're able to log in in to the Windows 10 computer. Click the Close button when you're ready.

9. Microsoft will send some emails to the child's account. One will be a Verification email, which you, or your child, will need to click the link to activate the account. They need to log in to Microsoft online to complete the process. The other email will be an invitation to join the family account, which you also need to Accept.

10. Using the child account to join the family will send emails to you confirming the accepted invitation. Back at the Windows 10 Family & Other People window, you can now click the child's account and allow it to log in; or manage it via the Microsoft Family portal online, which we'll look at in the next tutorial.

Options When You Sign in to Windows

New technologies inside Windows 10 enable you to log in with a fingerprint reader if you have one and – in the future – you'll be able to use facial recognition too. But you can still set up a picture password or PIN to make logging in easier.

The Various Ways You Can Log into Windows 10

Whether you use a password, PIN, picture password or fingerprint to log into Windows 10 we've got you covered. Let's take a look at the different ways available to sign in to Windows 10, from the least to the most secure.

1. What You See: When you start-up Windows 10, you'll see the lock screen. If you used Windows 8, it's something you'll be familiar with. You can get other information displayed here including network and battery life information, and you can change what appears in Settings > Personalisation > Lock Screen.
2. Log into Windows: As soon as you click any key or tap on the lock screen you'll get this – the Windows logon screen. You can use your password, fingerprint reader, picture password or PIN if you've set one up. You can always use the Sign in Options button to use a different method providing it's set up on your PC.
3. Facial Recognition: If you've seen adverts for Windows 10, you'll have seen that it makes a big play of not needing your password to log in. The catch is that you need a special Intel RealSense camera to use facial recognition. Laptops will have this built-in, but few do as yet.
4. Verifying Identity: Future devices will be able to recognise who we are. This technology – along with the ability to log in using your fingerprint - is referred to as Windows Hello by Microsoft.
5. Sign in Settings: You'll find the settings that govern logging into Windows in the Accounts section of the Settings app. Here you can set up your PIN should you choose to, or set up a picture password. it's this latter option we'll look at setting up for much of the remainder of this tutorial.
6. Set Up a Fingerprint Reader: If your PC has a fingerprint reader or compatible RealSense camera, you'll see extra options in this Settings screen under Windows Hello. Click the Setup button to get started with

these and you'll run through a setup wizard. Next, we'll show you how to set up a picture password.

7. Your Password: As with every time you set up a new way to log into Windows, you'll be asked to provide your password. Passwords don't go away completely even if you specify a new way to log in; you'll still need it to log onto Windows services online, for example.

8. What is a Picture Password? A picture password can be used with a mouse or touchscreen, but it comes into its own when used with the latter. That's because it uses particular gestures to identify you and this isn't the easiest thing to do with the mouse. You define these gestures by 'drawing' them on top of a picture.

9. Any Image: You can use any image you choose. Next you need to do three gestures on this image.

10. Confirm and Finish: Once you've performed your gestures, you need to confirm them by drawing them once more with your finger. Some people find this a bit difficult, but once you get the hang of it, you'll be fine. If you're worried about being locked out of your PC then don't be – remember, you're always able to use your password or PIN as well.

Exploring the Windows 10 Options

Windows 10 settings are actually spread across a couple of different menus but the main settings can be accessed by clicking the Start menu button, where you should see them pinned in the folder list. If not you can search for 'Settings' using the Windows 10 search bar. You can pin the settings icon to the taskbar or Start menu for easier access.

- External Device Settings: This is where you come to manage all of your connected devices, from printers and scanners to your mouse and keyboard. Related settings are also found here, including Bluetooth and touchpad settings if you are using a laptop.
- Main System Settings: Here you can find settings and options for things like the Display, Notifications, Apps, Power and Storage. The About section contains lots of information about the hardware in your computer as well as the operating system software version being used.
- App Settings: This is where you can find details on all of the apps you have installed on your Windows 10 computer. The main list shows you the name, file size, developer and the date it was installed (or updated). You can also set app preferences here, so which apps are used to complete certain tasks.
- Cortana Settings: Since the Fall Creators update you can access the Cortana settings through the main settings panel, rather than just through the Cortana sidebar. There are some new settings to find here since the update, including the ability to manage cloud search options.
- Privacy Settings: The privacy settings contains sections for all of the main areas where your privacy may be compromised, including some

which might not be obvious at first. Click on each of the section headings to see additional settings and options.

- Account Settings: Account settings contains all of the options you need for managing your local Microsoft account. This includes the secure sign-in options such as password, PIN and picture password, as well as the new Dynamic Lock settings, workplace or school access settings and Microsoft Family settings.

- Phone Sync Settings: A new addition with the Fall Creators update is the ability to link your Windows, Android or iOS phone to your PC and share documents, files and data more easily between them more easily. This section of the settings lets you set up the phone sync, and manage it afterwards.

- Network & Internet Settings: If you are having problems with your Internet connection, this is where you should come to find details and information. Everything from Internet options to flight mode and firewall settings can be found here. Each section contains links to more advanced options.

- Personalisation Settings: Nearly everything about the way Windows looks can be customised to some degree. Personalisation settings include options for changing the desktop wallpaper, colours of menus and windows, lock screen settings and the theme management tools.

- Ease of Access Settings: Previously called Accessibility, if you have additional accessibility needs to use a computer efficiently, you can find lots of settings here to make life easier. From a narrator tool and screen magnifier, to closed captioning and mouse and keyboard settings. You can even make the cursor thicker and easier to see.

- Gaming Settings: A new addition to the settings with the recent update, here you will find the newly added gaming tools. These include a game recorded (Game DVR), the tools for broadcasting your games and the Game Mode option. This helps to optimise any games you play on your PC.

- Time & Language Settings: In addition to the obvious settings for the time and date displayed on your computer (having this information correct is more important than many think) this is where you come to change the display and input language for your computer.

- Update and Security Settings: It is important to make sure that your Windows computer is up-to-date with all the latest updates and revisions. Within this settings menu, you can check to see which updates are available to download and install. You can also create backups and recovery discs here.

PIN THE SETTINGS

To pin the settings icon to the taskbar, click on the Start menu and then right-click on the Settings icon (the cog-shaped icon) and choose 'More…' Then click Pin to Taskbar. The Settings icon will now permanently appear in the bar at the bottom of the screen.

How to Keep Windows Up-to-date

Keeping your Windows 10 computer up-to-date is important for several reasons. First, major updates such as the Anniversary update, will add new features and second, smaller updates usually fix problems, close security holes and add improvements.

Checking for Updates

If you think that your PC needs to be updated, you don't need to wait for the automatic update process to kick in. You can quite easily check for updates yourself.

1. You can find the Windows 10 update information in the main settings app. Tap the Windows Key or click the Start menu button and then select the Settings icon from the side of the menu. Click the "Updates & Security" heading in the menu to open the relevant settings screen. If you don't get the home screen right off the bat, you can get there by clicking the "Home" button on the top left corner.
2. At the top of the window you should immediately see a message telling you whether Windows 10 is up-to-date or if updates are currently available. Directly below this message is a button labelled "Check for updates". Even if the message says up-to-date, it is worth clicking this button.
3. Any available updates will now display at the top of the window and the Check button will change to an Install button. You can install the updates straight away, but you will need to restart your PC after the install is complete, or you can reschedule to a more convenient time.
4. If you want to check which updates have been installed, perhaps if you need to confirm a security update for work, you can easily do so by clicking the "Update History" link directly below the Check for updates button. Updates are displayed, with more info available by clicking.

Windows Update Settings

There are several additional and advanced options available which can make the whole update process quicker, easier and more efficient, which is always a good thing.

1. Active Hours: By setting your active hours, you can tell your computer when you will most likely be using it. If you have updates set to automatically install and restart, they will only do so outside of your active hours. Useful for ensuring updates don't lose you school or office work.

2. Custom Restart Time: When a restart is scheduled, this option is available to temporarily override active hours and schedule a custom time to finish installing the current update. You will still need to make sure your device is plugged in at the scheduled time.

3. Update Delivery: You can choose how Windows updates are delivered in the Advanced Options. Windows Update Delivery Optimization lets you get Windows updates and Windows Store apps from sources in addition to Microsoft. This can help you get updates and apps more quickly.

4. Automatic Set Up: Some updates require you to restart your PC and sign in to Windows in order to finish installing the update. Windows 10 can help prevent this from happening by allowing Windows to use your sign in info to create a special token. Go to Advanced update options > Use my sign-in info...

5. Uninstall Updates: If for some reason you need to uninstall a particular update, perhaps the update is causing some software to not behave properly, you can do so fairly easily. From the Updates windows, click Update History > Uninstall Updates and use the interface to remove the update.

6. Windows Insider: As a beginner, you probably aren't too worried about seeing updates before they are released to the general public but this is exactly what the Windows Insider program lets you do. By joining the Insider program, you are potentially helping in the development of Windows 10 and beyond.

Exploring Start, Action Center and Taskbar

The Start menu, taskbar and Action Center are likely to be three of the most used areas of the Windows 10 interface for most people. There have been several additions and improvements to these tools in the recent updates, making them even easier to use, so let's take a look at what you can do with these essential Windows tools.

1. All Apps List: As you use Windows 10 and the various apps and software, a list of your most used tools will appear here. This is constantly updated as your use of the OS evolves. At the top of the All Apps list is a Recently Added section, showing newly installed software and a Most Used section showing your favourite applications. Click either heading to open a jump to letter menu.

2. Start Menu Folders: If you pin apps to the Start menu, their icons will appear below the block of tiles. You can now move these app icons into folders within the Start menu. To do this, click and drag one icon on top of another. If the bottom icon expands slightly rather than moving out of the way, drop the icon to create the folder.

3. System Folders: You can change the folders that appear in the bottom half of the Start menu, depending on how you use Windows 10. Settings, Power and All Apps will always be present in this part of the menu but everything else can be chosen in Settings > Personalisation.

4. Search Bar: The search bar is always visible to the right of the Windows button, unless viewing an app or game in full screen mode. Click in the Ask me Anything box and the search window will open. You can either type your search term or, if set up, use the Mic to ask Cortana. When

the search menu opens, it will hopefully be prefilled with relevant information and links.

5. Taskbar (left): The taskbar contains shortcuts to many of the most commonly used apps, including the Edge browser, App Store and File Explorer. You can add any app to the taskbar by right-clicking on the tile or app icon and selecting Pin to taskbar from the menu. Right-clicking on the taskbar will also allow you to add different toolbars to it.

6. Start Menu Tiles: Just as with Windows 8.1, the tiles that appear in the Start menu display information (when appropriate) from the apps and services they link to. You can customise the look of the tiles by right-clicking on them and selecting an option from the menu that appears. Tiles are now automatically split into relevant sections, e.g. Play and Explore.

Using the Main Windows 10 Start Menu

The Start menu in Windows 10 is useful for much more than just displaying a list of your apps and software. It includes Live Tiles, shortcuts to folders and settings, and you can even create folders within the menu itself. Learning how to use the Start menu is a must.

Get to Grips with Start

Microsoft has completely redesigned the Start menu for a new era and it seems to be improved with every update to the OS, so it takes a little getting used to at first. Here's our tour of the new Start.

1. You open the Start menu by clicking the Windows icon in the bottom left of the desktop or by pressing the Windows Key on your keyboard. The menu in Windows 10 is a mix of the Windows 7 and 8 styles but works better than either, with a list of apps on the left and Live Tiles on the right.

2. The live tiles work in the same way as they did in Windows 8. You can drag any of them around the menu should you wish to reorder them. You can right-click any file, folder or app in Windows 10 and select Pin to Start to include it here. Once in the menu, click and drag to rearrange tiles.

3. You can right-click anything in the live tiles area of the Start menu to bring up the tile menu. This lets you resize, unpin and even turn the live tile into a static tile. There are up to four different sizes of live tile: small, medium, wide and large, giving you lots of ways to build the perfect Start menu.

4. The tiles are split into groups. You can click the headings on existing groups to rename them. Dragging one of the tiles to the bottom of the menu, to an unused area of the menu, enables you to create a new group. A bar will appear at the bottom to indicate that a new group will be created.

5. The Start menu now allows for the creation of folders. This means that you can further organize the menu by keeping related app icons in a single place. To create a folder, simply click and drag an app icon over another. The icon beneath will expand slightly. Drop the dragged icon and the folder is created.

6. On the left-hand side at the bottom, there's a list of key items, such as the Settings app and a shortcut to the File Explorer. Click the power icon and you can shut down or restart your PC. You can add more options to this shortcut section in Settings > Personalisation > Start > Choose which folders appear.

7. The final area of the Start menu is the apps and software list. This displays all of the installed apps and software on your computer (software which doesn't require installation to run won't be shown here). Scroll up and down to view the full list and click the arrow next to apps to see more options.

8. The Most Used section at the top of the list enables you to access recently opened programs. This will also show recently opened files, so if you have Microsoft Word installed, simply go to the menu next to the icon in the most used apps menu and you can instantly open your recently worked upon files.

9. Clicking on any of the headings (including the individual letters) of the apps list will open an A-Z selection menu. You can then quickly click on any of the letters to skip directly to the listed apps that begin with that letter, rather than having to scroll down through the entire thing.

10. Finally, Windows 10 also makes it easy to resize the Start menu. Move the mouse to the edges and resize handles will appear, so you can have it covering half your screen or a much smaller proportion. You can even set the Start menu to open full screen, by going to Settings > Personalisation > Start.

Action Center: Managing Alerts and Notifications

There have always been pop-up messages in Windows but now there is a centralised way in which these are viewed and interacted with. Called the Action Center, it is designed to work more like the notifications panel on a smartphone or tablet.

Exploring the Action Center

The new Action Center is a key interface element in Windows 10, providing you with access to Quick actions buttons as well as the notifications and alerts.

1. You can open the Action Center by clicking the speech bubble icon on the far-right of the taskbar or by pressing the Windows Key + A on your keyboard. If you hover the mouse pointer over the Action Center button, it will tell you if you have any new notifications.
2. Any notifications are grouped by app, with a heading showing which app they are from. Notifications will remain in the panel until you actively dismiss them or action them (click through to the apps).

3. Clicking on a notification will take you to the app that generated it. You can also interact with certain notifications within the Action Center panel. On this screen, you can see that the Calendar notification allows you to snooze it for various lengths of time.

4. You can also control whether or not an app sends notifications, or whether notifications are prioritised, from within the panel. Right-click on the app heading when a notification arrives and choose the desired option from the action menu that appears.

5. If you right-click on the actual Action Center button in the taskbar, you will see some different options in the action menu that appears. These include the option to turn on Quiet hours, show/hide app icons and show/hide the number of notifications on the button.

6. In addition to being displayed in the Action Center, notifications will create a pop-up window that appears at the bottom right of your screen. Clicking on these pop-up windows will also take you to the app that generated the notification (the Calendar app for example).

7. When you're done with the notifications on the menu, you can click the Clear All button at the top to dismiss them. In Settings > System > Notifications and Actions, you can choose the Quick Actions that appear at the top of the bottom panel in the Action Center.

8. A very useful addition to the Action Center is the Quick actions panel at the bottom. This allows you to quickly perform some key functions (or actions) such as connecting to Wi-Fi. You can expand or collapse this bar by clicking the relevant heading.

9. The Quick actions panel contains the Tablet mode button. Tablet mode automatically prepares the desktop for use with a touchscreen and your fingers; perfect if using Windows 10 on a touchscreen laptop or tablet. Upon activation you will notice an instant change.

10. Whether you are on a Windows tablet or a laptop, at some point you will probably need to shut down the Wi-Fi and Bluetooth (on an aircraft for example). Clicking Flight mode halts all wireless communication and places an aeroplane icon in your notifications area.

Taskbar: How to Quickly Switch Between Tasks

In previous versions of Windows, the taskbar was relegated to being an occasional tool. In Windows 10 it's back where it belongs, at the very centre of the desktop workspace. Some slight tweaks in both the Anniversary and Creators updates, have made it an even more useful tool.

Mastering the Windows 10 Taskbar

The taskbar has always been more useful than many users realise and with Windows 10 there are several new features and options that make it even more so. Let's take a look at them.

1. Explore the Taskbar: The Windows 10 taskbar runs the full length of the screen and contains several separate areas. These are, from left to right: the Start menu button, the Cortana/Search box, your Pinned Apps and the System Tools. You have the option to customize almost all of these areas of the taskbar.
2. Start Menu Button: Clicking this, as you will no doubt know by now, opens the Start menu. This is where you find all of the apps and software on your computer listed, along with Live Tiles and system folders. Right-clicking on the Start menu button opens a different menu, containing links to system tools like Task Manager.
3. Cortana/Search Box: The Cortana/Search box is completely integrated into the taskbar in Windows 10, so it is always visible and available. Just click anywhere in the search box to begin using it. If Cortana is not yet set up, you will be prompted to do so the first time you click in the search box, and occasionally shown tips.
4. Task View: The simple white outline icon next to the search bar is Task View. This is Windows 10's new way to switch between open apps and it's really rather good, providing you can get used to using it. Click to open or alternatively you can open the Task View by pressing the Windows Key + Tab.
5. Pinning Apps: A few apps and other software will be pinned to the taskbar when you first use your Windows 10 PC. You can add more as

and when you choose. To pin apps, right-click on the app icon anywhere you see it (Start menu for example), click More and then Pin to Taskbar. Shortcuts can also be pinned.

6. System Icons: If we were using a laptop here rather than a desktop, a battery icon would appear in the notifications area. There's also a link to further settings, taking you to the appropriate area of the all new Settings app. The exact icons that appear here will vary depending on your system set up and apps installed.

7. Notifications: The Action Center gathers together all your pop-up notifications from things like the email app or Windows update. It also features Quick Settings buttons for things like Wi-Fi. The Anniversary update added notification badges, meaning you can see how many unread notifications you have.

8. Peek: Hovering over any open app icon in the taskbar brings up a Peek preview of the window. If a movie is playing, for example, you will see it playing here too. If you mouse over the preview, the X icon appears so you can close the window down directly from the taskbar should you wish to.

9. Taskbar Tools: The taskbar contains several unique tools. These can be shown or hidden as you prefer. They include the People app, Task View, the Windows Ink workspace and the Touch keyboard button. Right-click anywhere on the taskbar and you can show or hide these tools in the menu that appears.

10. Jump Lists: Right-clicking anything on the taskbar once again brings up a context menu. Apps such as Word and Excel feature jump lists, showing you recent files that you can pin to the list using the drawing pin icon. What appears in the jump list varies between apps, e.g. Chrome will show recent websites visited.

File Explorer: Exploring the Windows File Manager

The File Explorer is much the same as it was in previous versions of Windows but it is still worth you exploring it. The File Explorer is one of the most overlooked tools in Windows but if you want to be able to find your accumulated photos, music files, and word documents without having to use Search, it is definitely something you should be familiar with.

1. File Explorer Toolbar: This tabbed toolbar contains all of the tools you need to manage the different files and folders you can view. The main tab is Home, which contains tools for pinning to the Quick Access pane in the Start menu, copying, pasting, moving and renaming files. Once you have selected a file or folder in the main pane, the tools become active.

2. Navigation Pane – Folders: The left-hand sidebar contains a list of different file folders on your computer. Clicking on any of the folders shown here will display the various files and folders inside, in the main pane. The list is split into sections, including Quick Access/Recent, OneDrive and This PC. If you right-click on a blank area, you can choose to show All Folders here.

3. Info Bar: The thin bar along the bottom of the File Explorer displays several bits of useful information. If nothing in the main window is selected, the info bar shows the total number of items in the selected folder. Click on a file and the file size is also shown here. If you select

several files, the number of items selected is shown, along with the total size of all selected items combined.

4. Window Controls: Almost every window that opens in Windows includes these controls. From left to right they are: Minimise, Maximise and Close. Just below the standard window controls is a small arrow and a question mark. The arrow is used to show and hide the File Explorer toolbar, which is useful for smaller displays. The question mark will, when clicked, open a help page.

5. Preview Pane: If the preview pane is enabled, approximately a third of the File Explorer window and indeed, any other folder that you open will be reserved for a preview of any selected files. Normally, only image, html and text files will display a preview in this pane. The preview pane can be increased or decreased in size by clicking and dragging the scroll bar to the left of it. You can turn it on/off in "View" menu on the file explorer toolbar.

6. Folder View: The two buttons here let you choose between viewing the contents of the folder in a thumbnail format or alternatively, as a list. When the folder items are displayed as a list, you can choose to display a varying amount of information, including date last modified, file type and file size. Items shown as a list will still display a preview in the Preview Pane when selected.

7. Folder Contents Pane: When a folder is selected in the File Location sidebar, its contents are shown in the main pane. The contents of any single folder may vary greatly of course but Windows uses standard icons to show Word documents, text files, various different image formats and shortcuts to apps and software. As you can see here, images will usually be displayed as a thumbnail unless view settings have been changed.

File Explorer: Learn How to Navigate Windows 10

Here we'll take you through the improvements to the general Windows 10 file browser. Many features remain from Windows 7 and 8 (such as clicking in the far right of the taskbar to minimise everything) and apps on the taskbar work the same.

What's New in File Explorer?

File Explorer is a much undervalued part of Windows. And while it hasn't fundamentally changed for several versions of the operating system, Windows 10 introduces some interesting enhancements, which we'll take you through here.

1. The way you browse files in Windows 10 is broadly similar to previous versions of Windows, but File Explorer has been enhanced. The main Quick Access window shows you your most frequently used folders (after all, how many of us dip into more than five or ten folders in a day?) and also recent files.

2. The sidebar also works on the same principle and via a new Quick Access feature you can pin folders or files that you want to stick around. It will also show you Frequent folders too. You can pin things permanently onto Quick Access by right-clicking them and selecting Add to Quick Access.

3. There are also new icons across all File Explorer views, while there are a lot more file operations that you can access on the menu at the top of the window (known as the 'ribbon' in Microsoft speak) without the need to use the right-click menu. This is to make it easier for PCs with touchscreens.

4. File Explorer's Share tab also gets a new treatment, with the Share logo (first introduced with Windows 8's Charm bar) now used for file sharing from all apps. You can choose to email a file straight from the File Explorer window, add it to a zip file or share it with other Windows users.

5. If you want to see what other options you have for sharing – perhaps using the Windows Mail app - highlight the files you want to share, then

click Share. A pop-up bar will appear on the left of the screen and will show you the options you have to share that file(s) or folder(s).

6. The Windows 8 Charm bar has been abandoned in Windows 10 and the functions for Windows Store apps are hidden away inside the apps themselves; functions such as the Settings for the app itself and the ability to Print or Share.

7. If you've come from an earlier version of Windows, you might not be familiar with OneDrive. It's Microsoft's cloud storage application and it's available right from File Explorer in Windows 10, so you can access your files just as if they were on your own computer.

8. On-screen notifications have changed in Windows 10. Unlike in Windows 8, where they display in the top right of the screen, all notification action is now centred on the bottom right. There's also a place where notifications reside after they've popped up.

Folders: Create and Manage Desktop Folders

Despite all of the changes to the Windows OS, folders have remained as one of the core tools for organising your files. Much more than just boxes to keep your photos or music files in, folders can really help to improve how you use Windows 10 on a day-to-day basis.

Creating New Folders

It may sound too simple if you are a long time Windows user but here's a look at how to create new folders on the desktop and within other folders.

1. On the desktop, right-click and select New folder from the action menu that appears. The familiar yellow folder icon will then appear at that position on the desktop (wherever you clicked), with the name automatically set as 'New folder' but highlighted ready to change.
2. You can leave the name as 'New folder' if you wish. If you then create a second folder next to the first, it will automatically be named 'New folder (2)'. You can rename a folder at any time by left-clicking on the title once, or right-clicking and selecting Rename from the menu.
3. Double-click any folder to open it and view the contents. You can move items into a folder by selecting, dragging and dropping into an open folder or a closed one. If the folder is closed, drag the selected items over the top of it until the folder is highlighted, then release.
4. To delete a folder, right-click on it and select Delete from the action menu. You can also click and drag the folder to the Recycle Bin icon on your desktop. Anything in the folder will also be placed in the recycle bin. To move folders around the desktop, just click, drag and drop them. Use shift+delete if you wish to permanently delete a folder, skipping the recycle bin.

Managing Your Folders

Once created, folders can be adapted and customized in a number of ways. You can even change the default icon used whenever a new folder is added.

1. You can manage a folder in a number of ways without even opening it. Right-click on any folder and the action menu appears. The exact options that appear will depend on the apps or software you have installed but can include scan for viruses, compress, shred, zip and more.
2. The standard (Windows 10) options in the folder action menu include Pin to Quick Access, Open, Share With, Pin to Start, Send To, Cut, Copy and Create Shortcut. If there is a small arrow next to an option in the menu, it means a further options menu will open when rolled over.
3. Open the folder and a whole range of further options are available along the top of the new window. You will see four main tabs along the top: File, Home, Share and View. Each one of these, when clicked, will display a different set of further options relevant to the section.
4. Most of these options are self-explanatory, such as copy, paste and select all but some are a little more confusing. Most casual computer users won't need to use 90 per cent of the options in their day-to-day use but it is worth understanding them anyway. Add a few files to the folder and experiment.
5. If you want to get really deep into managing your folders, there are even more options to explore. Open any folder and right-click anywhere inside the main window. From the action menu that appears, click Properties. Here you can manage all sort of things, from security to icon style.
6. To change the icon style, that will change the style of all folder icons, click the customise tab and then click Change Icon at the bottom. Scroll to view all of the available icons (downloaded icons can be accessed by browsing), click on your preferred icon and click OK.

Task View: Learn How to Multi-task in Windows

Windows 10 has taken huge steps towards creating an OS which is suited to everyone, including busy multitaskers. It's easier than ever to switch between tasks in Windows 10 with Task View and you can even have extra workspaces for working in different apps.

Using Task View

Task View is a quick way to view and manage all of the windows and apps open on your PC at any given moment, even those that are minimised.

1. Task View is located next to the Windows 10 Search Box, identified as a filmstrip type icon. It has changed recently, due to the Spring Update, and now incorporates both Task View and the Timeline features. Don't worry if your icon is different, it could be because the latest update hasn't been applied yet. The functionality is the same, however.
2. Click the Task View icon, or press the Windows Key + Tab, to bring up the Task View and Timeline display manager. The display shows the current open and active apps on the system. It remains in this view until you click one of the active apps or press Windows Key + Tab again to switch back to the desktop.
3. In addition to clicking on one of the apps you want to launch, you can also flick between them using the arrow keys and hit return on the one you want. What's more, you can also close apps from here too: as you hover over with the mouse, a cross appears.
4. If you're used to using Alt + Tab to flick between apps then don't worry, this feature is still enabled. However, as in previous versions of Windows, it's just for switching. Even though it looks like Task View, Alt + Tab just switches apps, it doesn't enable you to close them.

Using Virtual Desktops

Virtual Desktops is a Linux feature that Microsoft has adopted for its more recent versions of Windows. It's a great way of separating apps across multiple desktop spaces and helps you concentrate and split your workload.

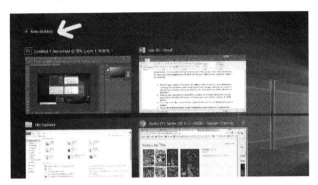

1. One of the great features in Task View is the ability to add extra desktops. Virtual desktops are essentially extra workspaces, so for example you can have one space with your email and chat windows open and another where you're working on a PowerPoint presentation without email distraction.

2. Click or tap the New Desktop button and you can see an entirely blank desktop like this. Don't worry, you haven't just lost all the apps that were on your screen before, they're on the other desktop.

3. You can go back to the previous desktop using the Task View button and clicking on the previous desktop.

4. You can also drag apps between the open desktops by dropping them onto the appropriate desktop icon. An app can only reside on one desktop at once, so clicking an icon on the taskbar or Start menu could flip you between desktops if the app is open elsewhere.

5. If you hover over the desktop icons, you can see an X appear; now you can close superfluous desktops down to save resources. Doing this doesn't close any apps down but it adds them to the oldest (original) desktop. They're called virtual desktops for a reason.

6. Virtual desktops are great for having different areas for different tasks. However, if you wish, you can select certain apps and have them appear on all open desktops. To do this, open Task View, right-click on an app and choose Show window on all desktops or Show windows from this app.

Timeline: Manage Your Activities

One of the most useful additions to the Windows 10 OS in the Spring Creators update is Timeline. This handy feature allows you to more easily get back to stuff you were working on previously, without having to have dozens of windows left open all over your computer. You will only see the Timeline features when you click the Task View button if you have the latest update installed.

1. New Desktop: Just as with the old version of Task View, there is a button to add extra virtual desktops. Virtual desktops are essentially extra workspaces, so for example you can have one space with your email and chat windows open, and another where you're working on a PowerPoint presentation without email distraction.
2. Task View: Timeline introduces a new way to resume past activities you started on the current PC, other Windows PCs, and even iOS/Android devices. The feature enhances Task View, allowing you to switch between currently running apps and past activities. The default view of Timeline shows snapshots of the most relevant activities from earlier in the day or a specific past date.
3. Earlier Today: The Earlier Today panel shows the latest activities on your Windows 10 PC. Documents you have viewed, apps you have opened, and websites you have visited can all be displayed here as a thumbnail image. Click on any of the thumbnails to be taken back to that app, document or web page.
4. Annotated Scrollbar: A very useful annotated scrollbar makes it easy to get back to past activities in Timeline. The scrollbar will change to

display dates, days or even times within a single day. You can scroll the Timeline screen using the arrow keys on the keyboard, or by clicking and dragging on the scrollbar.

5. All Activities: There's also a way to see all the activities that happened in a single day—just select See all next to the date header. Your activities will be organised into groups by hour to help you find tasks you know you worked on that morning, or whenever. And if you can't find the activity you're looking for in the default view, search for it.

6. Activities: In Timeline, a user activity is the combination of a specific app and a specific piece of content you were working on at a specific time. Each activity links right back to a webpage, document, article, playlist, or task, saving you time when you want to resume that activity later.

Notifications: Manage Notifications in Windows 10

If you've used a modern smartphone, you should be all too familiar with Notifications and alerts. Windows 10 has embraced the use of similar notifications in a much bigger way than older versions. Here's how to manage those useful little pop-ups and alerts.

Viewing Notifications

Viewing your notifications is very straightforward, as they are all grouped together within the Action Center. You can see when you have new notifications by the numbered badge that appears.

1. Some notifications pop up in a small window in the bottom right corner of the screen as they arrive, others will simply arrive in the Action Center and display a badge on the Action Center button, again at the bottom right of the screen. To see your active notifications, click the Action Center button.
2. Notifications are displayed under relevant headings and will be grouped together accordingly. So if you have two different Calendar app notifications, find them grouped together under a calendar heading. Notifications that pop up a window will vanish after a few seconds if you ignore them.
3. Some notifications can be interacted with in the pop-up or in the Action Center. For example, after installing an app such as Spotify, a notification will appear telling you that the installation was successful, and letting you launch the app or pin it to the Start menu straight away.
4. Notifications of events from the Calendar app will always appear as a pop-up first and then appear in the Action Center. You have the option to interact with both, by snoozing the notification for a selectable period of time. Doing this will remove it from notifications until it pops up again later.

Managing Your Notifications

You have a high level of control over how you are notified of things happening or requiring attention on your Windows 10 computer. Let's take a look at managing your notifications.

1. Notifications that are showing in the Action Center will disappear after you have clicked on them or actioned them. You can also remove them from the panel by hovering your mouse pointer over them and clicking the X that appears. Some notifications can be safely ignored, but be wary about which.

2. Right-clicking on a notification heading in the Action Center will bring up a small action menu allowing you to choose to turn off future notifications from that app or service, or make it a priority. You can also go directly from this action menu to the main notifications settings.

3. Right-clicking on the Action Center button will bring up a small options menu, allowing you to turn on/off Quiet hours (a period when no notifications are shown), whether app icons are shown in the Action Center and whether the number of notifications is shown on the Action Center button.

4. Open the main Settings > Notifications & actions and you can see several more ways to manage your notifications and the Action Center. At the top you will see the panel for reviewing, adding and removing Quick actions buttons (that appear in the Action Center). Available Quick actions will vary.

5. You will also see a few sliders that allow you to control general notifications settings such as whether you get notifications from apps, notifications are shown on the lock screen of your PC and whether they are shown when you are duplicating the screen.

6. Below these are sliders to enable or disable notifications for individual apps or services in Windows 10. Click on the name of the app or the feature and a new screen will open, letting you fine-tune the notification setting for each in much more detail (e.g. set the max number of notifications to show).

Desktop: Personalize and Customize the Desktop

One of the most welcome features of Windows 10 is the return to the familiar desktop environment and there are many ways to customize it to suit your needs and tastes; including icon size, background image and color scheme.

Change the Desktop Background

The Desktop personalization procedure hasn't changed much since Windows 7, so if you've used that OS before this will feel very familiar.

1. You can get started with personalising the Windows 10 Desktop in exactly the same way as you did with Windows 7. For anyone completely new to Windows, that means right-clicking anywhere on the Desktop screen and selecting Personalise from the action menu that appears.
2. The Background settings will be displayed first by default. Click the first drop-down menu to select whether to use the default backgrounds, solid colours or choose to display folders of your own images. Your choices here changes what is displayed in the background settings.
3. To select your own pictures for the background, click on the Browse button and navigate to the folder containing the images you want to use. For best results, you might need to crop some of your pictures to the same aspect ratio, i.e. widescreen, as your monitor screen.
4. To set a picture as your Desktop background, simply click on it. It will instantly be set as your new Desktop background image (a preview will display). The screen shows you the last five images used or you can click the Browse button to choose a new one from your folders.
5. If you opt for Slideshow, you will see some additional options to choose from. You can set the interval for the slide show from the 'Change picture every' menu and decide how you'd like the images to fit on the screen by clicking the 'Choose a fit' menu.
6. Even if you set a background image, you can also change the colour of the actual desktop. Click on the Colours option at the bottom and choose a background colour. You can also choose a custom colour from a more detailed hexadecimal colour selector.

Set Accent Colours

By accent colours we mean the colour of the taskbar, the Start menu and the frames of new windows and so on, that you open on your computer.

1. Apart from the desktop background, you can also change the colour of the taskbar and the Start menu and other system components. Click on the Colours option in the menu sidebar and choose an accent colour from the swatch. Recently selected colours are also displayed.
2. You can also let Windows automatically match the accent colour to the current desktop image. This isn't a perfect solution and works best if the desktop background image you are using is predominantly one colour. To do this, just tick the checkbox.
3. You can actually choose where the colour accent is applied. You can set it so it changes the Start, taskbar and Action Center and the Title bars of windows. You can also pick one or the other, or a combination of all options. You can also make these elements semi-transparent.
4. Since the Creators update, most of the core Microsoft apps allow you to choose either a light or dark theme (several have had this option for a while now). You can set the default app theme colour in the colours section of personalisation; this can be overridden in the app settings.

Lock Screen Customisation

The lock screen can feature custom backgrounds with Spotlight Images, display app statuses, and even give you direct access to Cortana.

1. The first thing to choose is whether to display one of your own images, a slideshow of images or something from Windows Spotlight. If you choose either of the first two of these, more options will appear to select the images you want to use (single or multiple).

2. You will see that there are two separate sections for adding apps here. The section with the single app icon is the one which will display more detailed information and the section with seven icons/spaces for adding apps which will show quick statuses.

3. You can add as many apps as you wish here, up to the maximum of eight. To choose which apps have statuses displayed, click on one of the spaces and choose from the pop-up menu that appears. The menu for the detailed information space will be slightly shorter than for quick statuses.

4. You can check how the detailed and quick statuses are displayed on your lock screen by letting your PC sleep or by pressing the Windows Key and choosing Sleep. Be aware however, that statuses may not show up straight away for things like Messages and Email.

5. There are several other lock screen customization options here. You can choose whether to display an image on the sign-in screen as well as the main lock screen and there are direct links to Cortana settings, where you can control how Cortana works on the lock screen.

6. The final two links take you to screen timeout and screen saver settings. The settings you choose there will depend on your personal preference and also on your computer location. Setting a shorter timeout means that your computer will be secure if you have to leave it.

Disable the Lock Screen

There is no setting to disable the lock screen completely but it is still possible to do by delving into the Registry. This is fairly advanced customisation, so approach with care.

1. To access the Registry, press the Windows Key + R, enter regedit, and then click OK. With the Registry open, navigate to HKEY_LOCAL_MACHINE\ SOFTWARE\Policies\Microsoft\Windows\. Right-click the final Windows folder and click New > Key.
2. Name this new key "Personalisation" and then navigate inside it. Right-click inside the right-hand pane and select New > DWORD (32-bit) Value. Name it "NoLockScreen". Then double click this new value and change the Value data to 1. Then click OK and exit the Registry Editor.

Adding New Themes

Themes can be added from a variety of sources but the best place to find them initially is the official theme page from Microsoft, or from the Windows 10 Store.

1. You can access the current theme page in a couple of different ways. You can open the web browser and navigate to www.support.microsoft.com/en-gb/ themes, or Google "Windows 10 themes". Alternatively, open Settings > Personalisation > Themes and click 'Get more themes in the store'.
2. All of these actions should bring you to the same themes page. Be aware that all themes here will soon be moved into the Windows Store app. Themes are listed in a variety of categories down the side of the page, ranging from Featured Themes, to themes with custom sounds supplied.
3. Each theme is displayed with a thumbnail and the number of images supplied shown. The Microsoft theme page doesn't allow you to view all of these images before you download, you just have to base your choice on the title and thumbnail. Click Download on any you like the look of.
4. Different themes will contain different amounts of content. Some might only have a colour profile and a few desktop wallpapers; others might contain icons, colours, wallpapers and sounds. Even the simplest of themes is likely to be more than just changing the desktop wallpaper.

Applying a Theme

A theme can spice up your desktop significantly, adding animations, custom icons and mouse pointers. Here's how to apply a desktop theme.

1. Once a theme is downloaded, you may need to open it to activate it. You can do this directly from the download interface that appears at the bottom of the browser window (showing download progress) or you can go to your Downloads folder, right-click on the file and click Open.
2. The theme will then be applied, and the first desktop wallpaper in the sequence will appear on your screen. Any colour profile changes will also be applied. If you want to manage the theme settings, head to Settings > Personalisation > Themes > Theme Settings.
3. Themes downloaded from the Windows Store won't need to be activated in this way. You can just click the Get button on the theme page in the store and then view the theme in settings > personalisation > themes. You can switch between themes here just by clicking the thumbnail.
4. Each theme applied can be customised further using the options in the Themes section. You can alter the background, colour, sounds and even the mouse cursor of any theme, making it completely unique to you. When you have chosen the changes, you will need to click Save Theme.

Change Your Desktop Icons

If you use desktop icons such as This PC, your personal folder or Network connections, you can change those icons. You can even download complete icon packs online, giving your desktop a completely different feel.

1. Open the Personalisation screen of the Settings menu and select Themes from the sidebar menu. You now need to look for the Related Settings option. In the Related Settings section, click on the link to Desktop icon settings.
2. The window that now opens lets you choose which default icons appear on your desktop. The Recycle Bin is just about essential but the others, including Computer, Users Files, Network and Control Panel icons are optional.
3. If you wish to do so, it is possible to choose different icons for these system tools and you can even download custom icons online. To change the appearance of the desktop icons, click on the icon you want to change and then click the Change Icon button.
4. The icon chooser window that appears will look very familiar to veteran Windows users, since it's essentially unchanged from Windows 98. Scroll through the gallery until you find an icon you like or use the Browse button to navigate to any icon pack you've downloaded.

Personalise Windows Sounds

You don't like the default Windows sounds? You want to replace them with all your favourite Star Trek sound effects? No problem!

1. To change the sounds that Windows uses to notify you about events and problems, open the Personalisation control panel as explained previously and click on Themes in the sidebar menu, then click on Advanced sound settings.
2. To change a sound, first select it from the list of sounds shown in the Sounds control panel, then click on the Browse button. Navigate to the folder containing the sounds that you want to use and then double-click the new sound. You can click on the Test button to hear what it sounds like.

Personalise the Start Menu

The final Customisation menu option lets you customise the Start menu to a limited extent.

1. You are presented with a list of toggle switches that activate certain options. The 'Use Start full screen' effectively returns you to the Windows 8.1 Start screen, so you'll probably want to leave it off unless you have a specific need for a full-screen menu.
2. Clicking on 'Choose which folders appear on Start' lets you choose from a list of preinstalled shortcuts to your Library folders. Choose only those you really need to have there; otherwise the Start menu can quickly become hopelessly cluttered.

Add Tools to the Desktop

If you want to take your customisation of the desktop to the next level, you can begin to add desktop tools such as Rainmeter.

1. Start by downloading the Rainmeter installer from the Rainmeter.net. To install the software, run the installer program that you downloaded and follow the instructions. You will have the choice to choose from the 32 or 64bit versions during the process.

2. The first time you run Rainmeter, your desktop will look something like the image here. Each small window on the right side of your screen (System, Disk, etc.) is a skin. This is the illustro skin set. The app remembers each skin's location and settings independently.

3. To move a skin, just click and drag it to a new location. The easiest way to interact with Rainmeter skins is through the context menu (right-click on the skin). A skin may have any number of tabs, buttons, menus or other bells and whistles in its design.

4. You can use the context menu to load skins from your library. Right-click on any of the skins and select illustro > Google > Google.ini. The Google skin will appear in the top left corner of your desktop. You can now drag it into place alongside your other skins.

5. You can also unload (remove) a skin with the context menu. Right-click the new Google skin and select Unload skin. You will see the skin fade away and disappear (useful for getting rid of the welcome skin). When a skin is unloaded, its location and settings are still saved.

6. Skins can have different variations. To see an example of one with variants, right-click the Disk skin and select Variants in the context menu. Variants share the same location and settings, and only one of a skin's variants may be loaded at a time.

Sticky Notes: How to Use On-screen Sticky Notes

There are lots of Windows 10 apps for making reminder lists but sometimes you just need a simple note to jog your memory. There is a simple and of en overlooked bit of software in Windows, that allows you to add sticky notes to your screen quickly and easily.

Adding Sticky Notes

The Sticky Notes software comes preinstalled with every version of Windows since Vista, although it has been improved slightly with each new release.

1. You can find the Sticky Notes software in the All Apps menu of Windows 10 or you can search for "Sticky Notes" using the search field in the taskbar. If you can't find it under S in the main All Apps menu, it might be within the Windows Accessories folder instead. Click to open the first note.

2. A blank Sticky Note will now appear on your screen. You will see that it looks just like a real Post-it Note, except the corners won't curl up and the glue won't fail. Click anywhere on the body of the note to make the cursor appear, if it isn't visible to begin with.

3. You can now type out your note. This can be a simple "Remember to call john", a shopping list (with the formatting added yourself) or any other simple note you might need. The note is not confined to the size of the original sticky note, with a scroll handle appearing if you reach the bottom.

4. You can resize the sticky notes, to make them slightly smaller or quite a bit larger, by moving the mouse pointer over the corner or edge until a handle icon appears and then clicking and dragging to the required size. This is useful if you don't want to scroll to see a longer note.

5. Once you have created one note, adding another is easy. Click the + button in the top left and another yellow blank note will appear. Repeat until you have enough notes. You can also right click on the icon in the taskbar and then New Note or use the keyboard shortcut Ctrl + N.

6. You can move the notes around the desktop however you wish, even overlapping them if required. Your sticky notes will stay in the position

you put them in, even when you shut down and restart your computer, as long as you don't close the software manually.

7. You don't have to stick to the default yellow colour note that you start with. Right click on any of your notes and then click the menu icon at the top and you can change the colour to a variety of presets. This is particularly handy if you want to make certain notes stand out.

8. You need to keep the app open for your notes to remain on the screen but as long as it is, you can shut down and reboot and the notes will remain on the desktop. To close notes, you simply need to click on the trash icon in the top right corner. Close the last note and the software closes too.

WINDOWS 10 ANNIVERSARY STICKY NOTES

Windows Ink, available for the first time in the Anniversary update, brings the writing you do every day into your digital world. Now, using a Windows 10 device, graphic designers can be more creative, musicians can write digital music, lawyers can edit documents with the power of the pen and students can make mathematical equations and learn by writing. All of this is available to any Windows 10 user, but even more useful for those with a touchscreen PC.

- Quickly and easily take a note, sketch on a screenshot or draw an idea.
- Smart Sticky Notes help you remember common tasks like reminding you of flight times or offering directions using Maps.
- Key apps have new Ink-specific features, like using handwriting in Office, Ink annotations in Microsoft Edge or drawing custom routes in Maps.

Browsers: Changing the Internet Browser You Use

The Edge browser is a great tool for surfing the Internet but it isn't perfect and it isn't yet as feature-rich as some of the more established browsers. Just because Edge comes preinstalled with Windows 10, doesn't mean you can't install a second browser to use.

Browser Choice

There are dozens of different browsers available, from the market leaders such as Chrome and Firefox, to more specialised offerings which focus on security or speed.

1. Google Chrome is a freeware web browser developed by Google. It was first released in 2008 for Windows and was later ported to most other platforms. As of September 2016, StatCounter estimates that Chrome has a 62 per cent worldwide usage share of desktop web browsers. Chrome is my personal favorite browser of all time.
2. Firefox, or Mozilla Firefox, has consistently been one of the fastest browsers around since its launch more than 10 years ago. Features include tabbed browsing, spell checking, incremental find, live bookmarking, Smart Bookmarks, a download manager, private browsing and location aware browsing.
3. Opera is a web browser developed by Opera Software. The latest version is available for Microsoft Windows, macOS and Linux. Opera includes built-in tabbed browsing, a bookmarks bar, add-ons and a download manager. Opera Speed Dial allows users to add an unlimited number of pages shown in thumbnail form.
4. If you really fancy something different, Torch is definitely niche. Torch is a Chromium-based web browser and Internet suite developed by Torch Media. Torch handles common Internet related tasks such as displaying media, sharing websites via social networks, accelerating downloads all directly from the browser.

Installing a Browser

Installing an alternative browser is very easy once you have decided which one to go for. Let's take a quick look at the process of installing Google Chrome.

1. To install Chrome for your user account, the first thing you need to do is download the installer file from https://www.google.com/chrome/ browser/desktop/index.html. Just click the big blue button and wait for the installation to finish.
2. When prompted at the bottom of the browser windows (where download progress is shown), click Run or Save. If you chose Save, double-click the installer file to start the installation process. Follow the steps shown on screen to complete this part of the process.
3. If you have used Chrome in the past, on a previous PC or before you installed Windows 10, you should have a Google account. Use this to sign in and Chrome will import all of your previous bookmarks, settings and extensions. Click Settings > Sign in to Chrome.
4. Signing in to Chrome connects your Google account to your browser for a more personalised browsing experience. All your Chrome data, like your bookmarks, history, passwords and other settings, is synced to your Google account and available on any device where you sign in to Chrome.
5. Most of the mainstream browsers offer some sort of account, so your information is saved, although few do this quite as thoroughly as Google Chrome. If you don't want to sync everything, you can also select which types of Chrome data you do.
6. You can customise Google Chrome to open any page for the homepage or start-up page. Your start-up page is the one that shows when you first launch Chrome on your computer. Your homepage is the one you go to when you click Home. Head into Settings and look for the relevant section.

Files: Learn How to Change File Associations

Windows 10 comes with its own default set of associations that open specific file types. A file association controls which apps or programs are set to open which types of files. If you're not happy with the default associations you can simply choose your own.

Default Programs and Protocols

The ability to change the default apps and programs that Windows 10 uses goes a long way to helping you take full control of your PC and the system software.

1. Click on the search bar on the left of the taskbar and type "default programs". You can also navigate to this settings tool by opening the All Apps list, scrolling down to W and clicking Windows System > Default Programs. Either way, open the tool on screen.
2. A list of apps already associated with various functions will appear. Click on any of these to see alternative options. The options shown will vary depending on the apps you have installed at this time. If a function has no apps associated with it, you can click 'Look for app in the Store'.
3. Below the description, you will see two options: Set this program as default and Choose defaults for this program. The amount of default file associations is also shown. Click 'Set this program as default' first.
4. Next, click on the 'Choose default apps by file type' option to see a list of all the file types that can be associated with your currently installed apps. These are the types of files which will automatically open in that app when clicked. Anywhere a + is shown, is without a default app.
5. You can also choose default apps based on protocols. This generally means that typing or accessing a certain URL will trigger the app to open, rather than a webpage. For example, if MAILTO is detected by the browser, our default email client (Thunderbird) will launch to handle the request.
6. Finally, you have the ability to set defaults by app, rather than choosing apps to go with certain files or actions. Click 'Set defaults by app' at the bottom of the screen. A new window will open, displaying a list of apps on the left. Click on any app you want to change the defaults for.
7. You now have two options: Setting the app as default for any and all files or protocols it can open, or choosing individual defaults the app will use. Clicking the first results in an instant change, clicking the second

will show you a list of current defaults for that app, allowing you to choose.

8. If you run into problems after changing protocols and defaults, you can easily reset to the Microsoft recommended defaults with a click of the button on the Default Programs screen. This may mean that you have to go back through your list and change some settings but it can be a useful fix.

Running Services

Being able to check which Windows Services are running at any particular time is also a useful option, as it can help to diagnose performance or stability issues.

1. The easiest way to get to the Services panel is by going through the Power User menu. Right-click on the Start menu button on the far left of the taskbar and select 'Computer Management' from the menu that pops up; this is the Power User or Win-X menu.

2. Click the 'Services and Applications' option in the left-hand panel of the window that opens. Then click 'Services' to show the full list. The list will be large but not all services will be running at any one time. Click on any to see more details, including management option, for that service.

Adverts: Learn How to Disable Annoying Adverts

Windows 10 has a lot of built-in advertising. This is part of the business model and is to be expected. That doesn't stop them being annoying. Thankfully, if you know what you are doing, you can disable most of the adverts that Windows tries to slip in front of you.

Disabling Annoyances

Windows 10 is pretty good at putting adverts in front of you and certainly, some of the adverts may not even seem like adverts until you start to take notice of them.

- Lock Screen Ads: Shortly after you enable Windows Spotlight for the lock screen, you will soon start to see the occasional advert for games like Tomb Raider appear among the pretty images. To disable the adverts, simply switch to the Picture or Slideshow options in the Personalisation settings.
- Suggested Apps: Windows 10 will occasionally show suggested apps in your Start menu. Sometimes these are free apps but often they are paid apps and games. Essentially, these are adverts. Head to Settings > Personalisation > Start and set the 'Occasionally show suggestions in Start' setting to Off.
- Get Rid of Fun Facts: Although Cortana will occasionally provide you with an interesting fact when you click the search bar; often they are interspersed with adverts too. You can disable 'Get fun facts, tips, and more from Windows and Cortana on your lock screen' in Settings > Personalisation > Lock Screen.
- Calm Cortana Down: Following on from the previous tip, you can also stop Cortana from doing that annoying thing when it bounces around in the taskbar to get your attention. If you don't want Cortana nagging you, click the Cortana search bar, click Settings, scroll down and disable the 'taskbar Tidbits' option.
- Microsoft Tips: Okay, so this might be classed as borderline as far as it being advertising but if you are fed up of being advised to 'Use Edge to save battery life', head to Settings > System > Notifications & Actions

and disable the 'Get tips, tricks and suggestions as you use Windows' option.
- Get Office Notifications: Windows 10 includes a 'Get Office' app that sits there, suggesting you download the software for a free trial period. Head to Settings > System > Notifications & Actions, scroll down and turn it off. You could also find the Get Office app in your Start menu, right-click it, and select 'Uninstall'.
- Disable Live Tiles: While you can remove the apps that are installed as part of the Microsoft Consumer Experience program, Windows 10 also includes a few apps you can't uninstall but will use the Live Tiles to advertise. To disable live tiles that annoy you, right-click a tile and select More > Turn live tile off.
- Unpinning Windows Apps: Rather than turning live tiles off, you can simply unpin the tile from the Start menu. Right-click a tile and select 'Unpin from Start' to get rid of the tile entirely. If you prefer a less cluttered Start menu, you can even choose to unpin all the tiles and only use the All Apps list to launch apps.

AD-BLOCKING SOFTWARE

The tips above will allow you to block many of the adverts Microsoft has added to the Windows 10 interface but what about the adverts you see on your favourite websites. Unfortunately, there isn't a Windows 10 setting to turn these off, but there is bit of software that can help.

AdBlock, with over 200 million downloads, blocks YouTube, Facebook ads and others in most places on the web. AdBlock works automatically but lets you choose to continue seeing unobtrusive ads, white-list your favourite sites or block all ads by default.

Internet: Connect Your PC to the Internet

Setting up your Internet connection is an important step in Windows 10. Joining and managing networks is easier than ever. One of the new features is Wi-Fi Sense that enables you to securely share network connection details with your contacts.

Manage Your Network Settings

We'll show you how to master your Wi-Fi settings and explain what you need to do if you have a problem connecting to the Internet in Windows 10.

1. Your Settings: Network and Internet is one of the key sections within the new Windows 10 Settings app. It features a plethora of settings for the different ways to connect to the Internet. While the Wi-Fi screen is fairly straightforward, there are different settings windows for Ethernet connections and even dial-up.

2. Wi-Fi Sense: We don't mind ourselves but some people are worried about the security implications of sharing network settings; or simply don't want to automatically connect to networks shared by others. You can disable it by visiting the right settings; just click Manage Wi-Fi Settings from the Wi-Fi window. You can also manage your known networks here.

3. VPN Settings: If you need to log into a corporate network, this is where you need to enter the appropriate settings. It's fairly easy to do but you'll need the configuration details from your IT helpdesk (they will have to enable you to have VPN access) plus your username and password.

4. Proxy Settings: If you use a proxy server, this is where you enter any specific settings to do with that. However, Windows 10 should automatically detect proxy settings. Note that the settings you configure here won't apply if you connect via a VPN, because a VPN is essentially a tunnel directly into the corporate network you're connecting to.

5. Your Usage: In a move designed to keep up with more mobile-based computing devices like the iPad, Windows 10 now includes a data usage page in Settings too. Here it splits your data between wired and wireless. We'd like to see more advanced settings than this too, so you could see how much data you used on a public wireless hotspot, for example.

6. Control Panel: Here we've left the Settings app and we're now in the Network and Sharing Center within Control Panel. The easiest way to get to this is to search for it or go to the Control Panel by right-clicking the Start button and selecting it from the menu. You can also get to it by right-clicking any network icon in the notifications area near the clock.

7. Sharing Settings: From the previous window, select Change Advanced Sharing Settings from the left-hand sidebar. You'll be taken to this screen where you can turn on network discovery; this governs whether your computer can see others on your network and whether you are visible to them. You can also turn file and printer sharing on or off.

8. Troubleshoot: From the Network and Sharing Center you can also click the Troubleshoot Problems button if you're having issues with connectivity and networking. Another way to troubleshoot problems with a Wi-Fi connection is to right-click the Wi-Fi icon in your Notifications area near the clock. Select Troubleshoot Problems from the menu that appears.

9. Disable Adapters: Another thing you can do is to disable and re-enable your network adapter (like the Wi-Fi card in your laptop). View your network connections by clicking Change Adapter Settings in the Network and Sharing Center and then right-clicking the network connection in question in the view above. Disable it and then re-enable.

10. Firewall: Another thing to bear in mind is the Windows Firewall. Normally you won't have any dealings with this whatsoever but if you're having problems accessing the Internet with a particular app, ensure it is listed here. Go to Control Panel > Update and Security > Windows

Firewall and then select Allow an App or Feature through Windows Firewall.

Edge: Exploring the Secure Edge Browser

Microsoft Edge lets you move quickly from browsing to doing. Write or type notes directly on web pages and share them with others, read online articles free of distraction and save your favourite reads for convenient access later.

- Browser Controls: Up in the top left corner, where you would probably expect to find them, are the browser controls. These include the button to add a new tab, the Page refresh button and the Page forward/Page back buttons. Right-click on the main tab and you will see additional options, including Re-open Closed Tab.
- Search Bar: There's no need to go to a website to search for pictures of adorable penguins or cute kittens. Stay put and save time by entering your search in the handy address bar. You'll get search suggestions, instant results from the web and your browsing history on the spot.
- News Feed: The main Home screen of Microsoft Edge is your News Feed. The news feed is provided by MSN and is made up of news stories based on your geographical location. If you are in the UK, the news will be from UK news websites, in the US, the news will be from American sources.
- Task View: The taskbar, which remains at the bottom of the screen when using Edge, contains a button that switches to Task View. Task View allows you to quickly view any open windows and folders, displaying them as thumbnails. This includes any open Edge browser windows.
- Customise Feed: You can customise the news feed to provide stories and articles that interest you personally. Click the "Customise" button and then choose your required location (UK, US, etc.). You can then click on the various categories, including: Entertainment, Money and Sport, and make them your favourites.
- Share: Windows Edge gives you more ways to share your discovered content than ever before. Click the Share button whilst on any web page and the Sharing panel will open. The title of the page will be displayed. Click this to choose whether to share a link or a screenshot. Then click the app you wish to share with.
- Web Note: Microsoft Edge on Windows 10 allows you to hand write notes on top of ANY website you visit. When you are on a website and want to add a written note, simply click the Web Note button. A new

menu bar opens, allowing you to choose pen colour and thickness. Now write your note and click Save.

- The Hub: The taskbar contains shortcuts to many of the most commonly used apps, including: the Edge browser, the App Store and File Explorer. You can add any app to the taskbar by right-clicking on the tile or app icon and selecting "Pin to Taskbar" from the menu.

Edge: Learn How to Use Microsoft Edge

Edge replaces Internet Explorer as the main Internet browsing tool in Windows 10. Edge is designed to be safe and fast and it boasts several innovative features such as the ability to set aside tabs and highlight parts of web pages and share them with others.

Get Started with Edge

Edge is fast and fluid and we think you'll like it. It may not have the capability of Chrome or Firefox as yet but for basic web browsing it's almost perfect.

1. Microsoft Edge carries on Internet Explorer's use of a stylised 'e' as its logo. This is to make things simple for users who are familiar with Internet Explorer. Click on this icon in the taskbar to open Edge or on the Start menu and find it in the All Apps list.

2. If you're familiar with almost any modern browser, you will instantly be at home. The forward, back and refresh panel is almost identical to other browsers. The default new tab page shows your most visited sites but you can have news from MSN appear instead.

3. As well as Edge's main controls in the top left, there are other items in the top right including the main menu to access more options. This is shown by the ellipsis (...) icon. From the main menu you can open a new window or a new InPrivate window as well as zoom into the current page.

4. You can begin using Edge by typing a search term or a complete website URL (address) in the search field near the top of the screen. Search results are then displayed in a fairly standard mixed list of links, images and videos. Click on any of them to see the website they link to.

Customising Microsoft Edge

Once you become accustomed with the basics of Microsoft Edge you can start to explore the many options and settings available for personalising and customising.

- Accessing the Settings: From this menu you're also able to access Settings as well as Print and Find, to locate a word or phrase in the open web page. Another option enables you to pin a particular web page to the Start menu as a tile should you wish to.
- Advanced Edge Settings: The basic Settings menu is pretty lean on options but an Advanced Settings button at the bottom takes you into another menu with further options. This part of Edge is for more advanced users and it covers privacy, such as enabling browser cookies and other security settings.
- Change the Edge Theme: As well as the 'light' default theme of Microsoft Edge, there's an option in Settings to display a black theme. It's becoming a lot more common for applications to have dark themes, with the Windows 10 taskbar dark too. It's a good alternative to having super bright apps.
- Change the Search Engine: Microsoft Edge is set to use Bing as its default search engine but you can change search provider in the Advanced Settings menu. As you type into Edge's search box, the browser recommends search suggestions. You can turn this off here should you want to. We find it quite useful.
- The Edge Sidebar: Again in the top right, the ≡ icon launches the sidebar featuring your Reading List, Favourites, Downloads and History. If you've used Internet Explorer at all recently, this sidebar will be familiar

to you as it's basically the same interface element. However, Reading List is new.

- Pinning the Sidebar: In the top right of the sidebar there's a pin to keep the sidebar open, rather than just temporarily. You can move easily between your Reading List, Favourites, Downloads and History; just use the icons at the top of the bar to select the one you need.

- Set Aside Tabs: You can now set tabs aside, rather than closing them completely, so that they are easier to go back to later. Tabs that are set aside should not take up bandwidth, so you don't need to worry about lots of open tabs slowing down your browsing. Tabs set aside are still there even after closing Edge.

- View and Restore Tabs: Tabs that are set aside can be viewed in the new Tab Viewer. You can access this by clicking the small down-facing arrow next to the New Tab button at the top of the window. Clicking any tab here switches to it. Alternatively, click the Tabs sidebar button at the top left of the window.

- Import Your Bookmarks: Edge now makes it easy to import bookmarks saved in another browser (Google Chrome for example). Quickly get your bookmarks, saved passwords and browsing history from other places on your PC by selecting More > Settings > Import from another browser, and then choosing the correct one.

- Read eBooks in Edge: The latest update to Microsoft Edge lets you read eBooks in .epub format. Books in this format automatically open in Edge when double-clicked. They can then be saved to the Reading List for easier viewing at a later date. Take a look at www.feedbooks.com/publicdomain for some freebies.

- Enable the Favourites Bar: One of the folders is called Favourites Bar. This is a bar you can toggle on and off to permanently display certain Favourites in a strip underneath the address bar. To enable this feature, go to Settings via the main menu and switch the Favourites bar on using the toggle.

- Annotating Pages: Making notes on web pages and sharing the results is one of the best new features in Edge. Launch this mode using the pen button next to the sidebar control in the top right of the main window. The editing controls include a pen, a highlighter, an erase function, an annotation feature and a copy tool.

Microsoft Edge Extensions

A new addition to the Edge browser in the Windows 10 Anniversary update is extensions. Extensions are small pieces of software you can add to Edge to give additional functions.

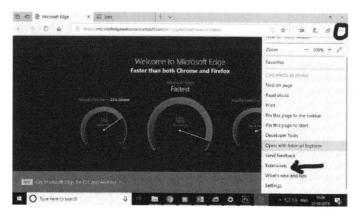

1. Open the Edge browser on your PC and look for the small Menu button at the top right of the window. Click this and then click the new Extensions link. When the extensions panel opens for the first time, it should be empty apart from a link to Get extensions from the Store.
2. Click the link and the Microsoft Store app opens, displaying the available extensions. There are not that many to choose from right now but more will be added as app developers learn to take advantage of this new Anniversary feature in Windows 10.
3. Click on any of the extension icons shown to open the information page. This tells you more about what the extension does, which devices it is available on and the minimum system requirements to run it properly. Scroll down the page to see user reviews and recommended extensions.
4. To begin installation of your chosen extension, click the Get button at the top of the page. This then changes to show installation progress which, depending on the size of the extension, should take just a few seconds. The button then changes to say Launch.
5. Clicking Launch will take you back to Edge with the extensions sidebar open. You then need to choose to enable the extension in Edge or keep it turned off for the present. Important information, such as whether the extension needs access to certain details on your PC is shown.
6. How you use your new extension depends on what it actually does. The one we installed here is for analysing the structure of websites, so when

we get to a website we want to examine, we have to click the Menu button and then select the extension from the list at the top.

Search: How to Search for Anything in Windows 10

Until you use it, it's difficult to put into words just how much better Search is in Windows 10 than in previous versions of Windows. Microsoft did have a lot of ground to make up to match the search functions on of er in rival operating systems such as Apple's macOS.

Windows 10 Search Basics

Search now not only finds files but settings, emails and apps too. You can even search for websites as well, providing you're happy with results from Microsoft 's own Bing search engine.

1. If you need to search for anything on your Windows 10 PC, the taskbar search bar is now the place to do it. You can still hit the Start button (or Start key on your keyboard) and start typing if you used to do that to search in previous versions of Windows.

2. In addition to files and folders, you can search for web results and apps. When you first click in the search box you will see three tabs along the bottom that lets you choose what to search for but even if you don't click one of these, the search function is smart enough to return results from all.

3. Search results are displayed in sections (best match, apps, folders, etc.) so that you know what you are looking at. Apps will be displayed with their icon next to them, folders will have a folder icon and images will be shown as small thumbnails within the search results panel.

4. You can further filter the results that have appeared after you search by clicking on the small arrow at the top of the results panel. This lets your filter by any of the possible, even music or video. Suggested search results can be previewed by clicking the right-facing arrow next to them.

Search Settings and Tools

You have quite a lot of control over exactly how search and Cortana provide you with search results, and what information they store about your search history.

1. Safe Search: Sometimes web search results may show content that is not suitable for the younger audience, which is the reason Cortana also offers search filters. Go to Settings > Cortana > Permissions and History, and under SafeSearch, select the search filter that is most appropriate for you.

2. Cloud Search: Cloud search is a new option, available with the Fall Creators Update, which allows you to suppress cloud content on search results. Under Cloud Search, you will see a toggle that says Windows Cloud Search. This option manages whether Cortana shows cloud content in Windows Search.

3. Device History: This setting allows for improvement of on-device search results, whether you are using an app, settings or another search from any signed on device. If you prefer that Windows does not record on-device search history, you can switch this option off in Settings > Permissions & History.

4. Search History: Search History can also help to provide better search results. It can also be turned off, just like the Device History. Head in to Settings > Permissions & History and use the toggle to turn it off. If you click Search History Settings a browser window opens showing the history.

5. File Explorer Search: You can always search for files and folders in File Explorer as you could in previous versions of Windows. With the new taskbar search you won't need to use this as often as you did but it's still there if you need it. We don't find it as quick as the taskbar search, though.

6. Searching in Settings: Windows 10 allows you to search for settings from within the Settings app. Open the app and you will see the search box right at the top, underneath the window title. Possible results are displayed as you type, just like a normal search, but the results will only be from settings, nowhere else.

Cortana: Using the Built-in Personal Assistant

Cortana is Microsoft's 'virtual assistant'. If you've heard of Siri on the iPhone, it's very similar. You can talk to it and it will pick out relevant information that's appropriate for you. If that sounds like it's too much, we'd encourage you to give it a chance.

Meet Your Digital Assistant

The Cortana personal assistant could well be a completely new experience for many users. So we've gone into quite a lot of detail here in order to give you the complete picture on how Cortana can be of help to you day-to-day.

1. Welcome to Cortana: On the previous pages we talked you through Search in Windows 10. Cortana is like a layer on top of this search; you can either enable it or ignore it. Cortana isn't on by default in Windows 10. To enable it, click the Circle icon at the bottom of the Search sidebar.
2. Setting Up: Click Next. Basically, you'll need to allow Cortana to access all the information on the rest of your computer. It sounds alarming that you're enabling Cortana to look at your Calendar, browsing history and so on, but it needs to process this information to make things relevant for you.
3. Tell it Your Name: Now you'll begin a bit of further personalisation of Cortana so it understands your voice and, as here, knows your name. As the Microsoft statement said in the previous step, you can always change individual parts of what Cortana remembers (via the Notebook, which we'll come onto shortly) or disable it entirely.
4. Allow Location Access: As with virtual assistants on mobiles, Cortana works best when it knows where you are in the world. All our phones know where we are, so why not your PC? Unless you've a specific reason to forbid it, we recommend letting Cortana know your location.
5. Location Settings: If you're concerned about the amount of location access you're giving at any time, you can always disable Location completely in the Settings app. You're also able to decide what apps have access. If you want to turn it off temporarily, you can do this using the Location button at the bottom of the Action Center.
6. Set Up Your Microphone: If you want to talk to Cortana (or at least have the option to), you'll need to ensure it can hear you correctly. Here

we've got a problem with our microphone which we need to remedy. Many desktop PCs won't have microphones unless you have one in your webcam or another accessory, for example.

7. Get in Training: As with any app that requires talking to your PC, Cortana will take you through a little bit of training. It will adjust to your voice and the distance you are from your microphone. Some laptop microphones are especially bad, so Windows needs to compensate for that.

8. Back to Cortana: We've trained, we've configured and we've allowed Cortana full access. Let's see what Cortana has for us... Don't forget you can still use the search bar just as before. Cortana is another way to search, providing different information. It doesn't have to be seen as a replacement.

9. Your Interests: To finish the setup, Cortana will pick you a few starter interests. This changes the default content you'll see when you click the search box to bring up Cortana. Now, it's perfectly possible Cortana could pick you the wrong stuff. It's all part of the process as, if you correct it, Cortana will learn from its mistakes.

10. Changing Settings: So Cortana picked us out a batch of things including general news. To change these further, bring up the Cortana menu from the left-hand sidebar and bring up Notebook. Note that Reminders is a further useful feature; you can ask Cortana to remind you to go shopping at 12 or home at 5, it's completely up to you.

11. Your Notebook: As you can see, your Notebook (we don't think it's a particularly accurate name) contains various interests that Cortana will show you information about, as well as access to Cortana's settings (more on those shortly) and your personal information. Connected Accounts will show other things Cortana is connected to, like Microsoft Office.

12. Change an Interest: If you want to disable or enable an interest for Cortana, click that particular option. You'll then see a window like this one, which enables us to enable or disable the interest as well as fine-tune the details. In this case, we can select which stocks and shares we'd like Cortana to show us.

13. The Main Cortana View: So we've gone back to the main Cortana window, where we're shown some automated content we'll talk you through in a second. Once again, if you start typing or say something if

you've got voice set up, this automated content will disappear in favour of the Search menu.

14. Popular Now: If you scroll down the Cortana window there are other things for you to browse through, most of it powered by Bing, Microsoft's web portal, which gathers news and entertainment from various sources. There's an area for articles that are popular now and you can click through to anything that's of interest.

15. Eat and Drink: If you selected the oddly-named Eat and Drink as an interest, you'll see restaurant settings from Yelp or Foursquare. In the settings you can say how often you like to go out, what your budget is and how far you usually like to go. Most useful for regular business travellers, we'd have thought.

16. Weather: Probably Cortana's most used feature is that it will present you with weather for your current location. Clicking on it for more information will launch the Windows 10 Weather app (which is rather good, so no problems there), although the basic forecast should be enough for most needs.

17. "Hey Cortana": in Settings, you can turn Cortana off completely as well as choose whether it should present you with flight and other transportation information. To track this Cortana will read your emails! There's also the option here to have your device constantly listening out for Cortana requests beginning with 'Hey Cortana'.

18. Speaking to Cortana: So if you enable it, saying 'Hey Cortana' will wake up Cortana. You'll see the search box jump into life and you can then launch into your question pretty much straight away. Alternatively, you can just click the microphone icon on the right-hand end of the search bar.

19. Asking Natural Questions: The idea is that you should be able to ask Cortana quite natural questions. Here we've asked what the weather will be like at the weekend, but you could equally ask if you'll need your umbrella. You can also ask specifics like "where is good round here for chinese food?".

20. Find a Setting: Of course, asking natural questions also means you can ask about where things are on your PC. If you're willing to talk to your PC, you can really speed things up.

21. Pipe Dow: Finally, it's worth mentioning one further setting, towards the bottom of the menu. Called Taskbar Tidbits, having this enables

Cortana to greet you with a phrase in the search box – mainly to encourage you to use Cortana. It's not a big thing, but it could be irritating to some, but you can turn it off should you wish!

Mail: Explore the Email App in Windows 10

Long gone are the days of Microsoft Outlook Express being included with new releases of the OS, replaced instead by the Microsoft Mail app. This app first appeared in Windows 8, was vastly improved in 8.1 and has now been improved yet again for Windows 10. Just typr "mail" in the search box and you'll see it. Add your mail account to it and you're good to go!

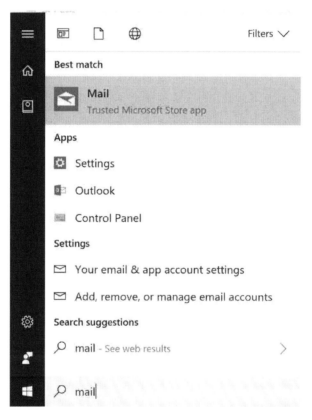

- New Mail Button: If you are not replying to an email, but rather starting a new email, you can do so in a couple of different ways. You can either click the New Mail button at the top of the Mail Menu or you can use the Ctrl-N. Both methods open a new email in the main window, with a blank recipient field.

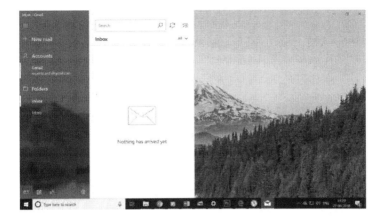

- Mail Menu: The left-hand menu, which can be minimised and expanded using the button at the top of the panel, contains all of your email accounts (those you have added to Windows Mail). Click on any of your email account headers and the individual folders, such as Inbox and Sent Items, are displayed here also.

- Calendar View: You can open the Windows Calendar app directly from within the Mail app. Click the Mail app icon at the bottom of the Mail Menu panel and the calendar screen will open in a second window. If you have never used the Calendar app before, you will need to link it to an account.

- Mail Settings: The settings for the Mail app allow you to easily add accounts, change how emails are displayed when they arrive, whether outgoing emails have a signature (which can be customised) added to them, as well as how you are notified of new emails in Windows 10.

- Mail Folder: The messages in whichever email folder you have selected are shown in this panel. By default, the most recent emails are at the top of the list. You can change how the emails are viewed, so that only unread or flagged emails are displayed, using the dropdown menu at the top of the inbox.

- Message Options: In a row along the top of the main message window are the message options. These include Reply, Reply All, Forward, Archive and Delete emails; more options can be seen by clicking the Menu button to the right. The message options only appear when viewing a received message.

- Message Tools: Roll over or click on any of the messages in your inbox, sent items or drafts folders and three icons will appear. These let you quickly Archive, Delete or Flag any message directly in the folder panel. Archived messages can be recovered at any time and returned to the inbox if required.

- Main Message Window: When you start a new email or select an email in one of the mail folders, it will appear in the main message window. As you would normally, you can scroll down to view all of the messages shown. You can roll over the address in the To: field, to see more contact details.
- Taskbar Icon: Whenever you open an app in Windows 10, a highlighted taskbar icon will appear at the bottom of the screen. This makes it easy to switch between multiple open apps, or to quickly see which apps are currently running. You can pin your most used apps to the taskbar by right-clicking and selecting Pin to Taskbar.

Mail: Setting Up and Using the Mail App

Windows 10's new email client is a lot different from previous apps such as Outlook Express. It's a relatively recent idea for you to have all our email in one place, whether it's your work account, a Hotmail or Outlook address or email from Gmail.

Meet Your New Email Client

Mail has been completely redesigned for Windows 10 and is wholly unrecognisable from the Windows 8 equivalent (that's a good thing). But even with these improvements, it still needs a bit of tweaking before it comes into its own.

- **Welcome:** As it says here, the idea behind the Mail app in Windows 10 is to gather all your emails together in one place to "simplify life a bit". The app is quite clever in how it handles email and it certainly differs to older apps such as Windows Live Mail and Outlook Express.
- **Default Account:** If you signed into Windows 10 with a Microsoft account, the Mail app will automatically pull this in if it's enabled for email. As you can see, you can also click Add Account if you have other email accounts you want to add (this can be from basically anywhere as long as it's your account).
- **Account Type:** If you click Add Account, you can add accounts from many popular providers including Google, Yahoo and Apple's iCloud. You can also set up other more specialist accounts if you have the details. Finally, there's also an option to add a Microsoft Exchange account if your workplace uses that (including Office 365).
- **Advanced Setup:** If you need to select the Advanced Setup option, you can choose between the type of account you're setting up. Usually you'll select the Internet Email option – this includes accounts that use the POP3 or IMAP protocols to retrieve email (if your provider gives you the choice of which of those to use, select IMAP).
- **Google Accounts:** If you're adding a Google account, you'll get this somewhat familiar pop-up appearing inviting you to enter your username and password. If you have Google's two-step authentication enabled, you'll get a text message to confirm your identity and you'll be asked to enter it.

- Microsoft Accounts: As we said before, your Microsoft account will hopefully have already pulled in automatically. If not, you can add it manually. Just enter your email address and password. We looked at Microsoft accounts in more detail on page 10, but if you want to sign up afresh you can do that here too.
- Your Inbox: Your email list is shown on the left, with the contents of each email appearing on the right. New emails are designated by the blue colour. You can also search for any emails using the search box at the top – this works much more quickly than in older apps.
- Writing a Mail: Click the "+" symbol on the top left of the app to write a new mail.
- Insert Attachment: Emails are 'grouped' like this in Mail, meaning that if you and a friend have a conversation, all the emails will be grouped together so that they're easy to retrieve. You'll notice we're still composing our email here, and we've clicked the Attach button to select an attachment.

- Sent Mail: Go to folders> Sent Mail to see your sent items.
- Edit Text: As well as just writing simple plain text emails, there are plenty more editing functions in Mail, which we'll check out in the next few steps. Using the Format tab at the top of the editing window, you can change selected text.
- Apply Styles: There are also various pre-defined styles you can apply to text – useful if you're writing a long email and you need to have sub-headings or headlines in the text. These work very similarly to styles in Microsoft Office; styles that you might use for a report or essay.

- Define Styles: You can browse through these styles using the drop-down arrow next to the style selection box. As well as fairly standard styles, there are some other ways you can get text to stand out including quotes and what are called 'Intense' styles, which place quotes in between parallel lines to encourage reading.
- More Text Options: As well as styles, Bold, Italic and Underline, there are other ways you can make text stand out or add emphasis. As in Word, you can have subscript or superscript text or add highlighting (quite useful for quick editing of paragraphs in emails). Finally, you can clear the formatting of any selected text.
- Change Colour: You're able to easily change the colour of the text in your email and, while you still have a limited range to choose from, you've still got a lot of choice (far more than in many other apps, anyway). Strangely Windows chooses to take most of these colours from your current Windows theme. No, we're not sure why, either.
- Inserting Images: As well as the button to include attachments, the Insert tab features a Picture button so you can insert an image into your email, as opposed to just sending it as an attached file. Once inserted, you can select it with your mouse and adjust its size (drag the corners as needed).
- Spelling Options: Before you send an email, you can always spell check it – this is integrated into Mail under the Options tab. You can select the language you need and correct any spelling errors as you go.
- Email Menu: As well as the basic reply, reply all, forward, archive and delete commands at the top of each email, there's also this extra menu – just click the ... button. You can move to the next email or previous message if you want to do that, but crucially you can also move your email into a folder.
- Move Folder: If you chose to move your email in the previous step, you'll see this browser view which enables you to add your email to an existing folder. You can always create a new folder for storing emails in particular categories. If you just want to remove your email from the inbox but still keep it, use Archive.
- Change Zoom: If the text in emails is too small for you, you can zoom in to your messages – again, this is also accessed through the ... menu. A handy keyboard shortcut for zooming in is Ctrl-+ to zoom in or use Ctrl

and – to zoom out. This actually works in most apps, including many web browsers, too!

- Right-Click: Even if you're not actually looking at a particular email, you can still perform numerous actions on it. You can right-click on emails to move, archive or delete them or mark them as read/unread. If you're deleting emails, you can also just select them and use the delete key (we find this is actually the easiest way).
- Print It Off: From this menu you can also print off emails – this will open the now-standard Windows print dialog box which is now black (presumably to make the predominantly white print preview stand out). You can select to print off the whole email or just the first page, as well as browse through the pages using the controls at the top.

Windows 10: Security and Privacy

While the Internet is a marvel of the modern age, it also has a dark side that's forever lying in wait for the unsuspecting user. Viruses, spyware, malware, ransomware and other digital threats are ever present but in this section you can learn how to best combat this unwanted side of the Internet. Learn how to defend your PC against viruses, secure your privacy, backup your important files and restore them in case of an emergency.

Antivirus: The Best Security and Antivirus Software

While the built-in Windows Defender is a great antivirus and security tool, it's nowhere near as capable as one of the many third-party security suites. The likes of Bitdefender, McAfee and Symantec have years of security specialism behind their products.

Better Protection

A third-party security suite of ers much more than virus scanning. Here are ten security suites worth considering if you're serious about your digital protection.

- Bitdefender: Total Security 2017 is the latest security suite from one the world's leading security specialists. This version offers unrivalled levels of protection and performance for Windows, macOS and Android platforms. There's even an advanced ransomware protection element to help protect your folders.
- McAfee: McAfee Total Protection offers a 100 per cent guarantee of virus removal, or you get your money back. There are three main versions available: Antivirus Plus, Total Protection and LiveSave; each has its own particular twist but all offer excellent security features and benefits. McAfee also offer mobile protection software.
- Symantec: Norton Security Premium is the top choice for the home user from Symantec. With it you can protect up to ten PCs, Macs, smartphones or tablets and it keeps you safe when shopping online, general surfing or when conducting transactions. Includes 25 GB of secure cloud storage for your PC and premium family safety features.
- Webroot: Perhaps not as well-known as big names like Norton or McAfee, Webroot offers three possible solutions, including Webroot Internet Security Complete. This is the best one to consider as a standard home user. With it you're protected from virtually any threat, as well as getting 25GB of secure online cloud storage.
- Panda Security: Panda Internet Security is designed to ensure you can enjoy your online life with complete peace of mind. It provides maximum antivirus and online fraud protection for your PC, the firewall and Wi-Fi protection. Control and safeguard access to your data, documents or any sensitive information. Includes parental controls too.

- Avast: Avast has offered free antivirus software for many years but its other products, Internet Security, Ultimate and Premier, are also well worth looking into if you need a little more protection. With all paid versions, you get online banking protection, identity protection and email protection; and all at a reasonable cost too.
- Emsisoft: Emsisoft Internet Security is an award winning security suite that offers plenty of great features and elements. It's quick, easy to use, cost effective and does an excellent job of protecting you and your devices from modern security threats. Offers surfing protection, real-time file guard, behaviour blocker and anti-ransomware.
- ESET: ESET Internet/ Cyber Security is a comprehensive protection package for everyday users. It offers online banking protection, alerts for any malicious attempts to control your webcam and is a fine-tuned balance between security and privacy. Allows you to test your passwords and scan your devices for vulnerabilities.
- F-Secure: F-Secure has been in the security and protection business for many years and as such, its products are often considered some of the best available. F-Secure Total is the top choice for the home user, as not only does it provide superb antivirus protection but also offers a Virtual Private Network (VPN) for added privacy when online.
- Trend Micro: Trend Micro Maximum Security offers superlative protection for up to five different devices along with extended protection for children, Internet passwords and privacy on social media sites. It's great value for money and performs excellently too. Trend Micro offers intuitive settings and clear, easy-to-understand status reports.

Defender: Using the Windows Defender Tools

Since a recent update, Windows Defender, the preinstalled security tool for Windows 10, is better than ever. Defender now includes automatic analysis of suspicious software. You can even run a powerful offline scan that can pick up nasties that a normal scan may not.

Set Up Defender

By default, Windows Defender should already by running but if you are using a PC that has had antivirus software on in the past, parts of it may have been disabled.

- The first thing to do is check that Defender is already running. You can quickly check this by clicking on 'Show hidden icons' (the small arrow button) at the right-hand end of the taskbar. If you see the Defender shield logo, you are protected. At least, you are protected partially.
- Now it's time to check out the Defender settings and features. You can right-click on the icon in the hidden icons pop-up, and then click Open. You can also, in the search box on the taskbar, type Defender and then select Windows Defender from the list of results.
- Since the Spring Update of 2018, Defender is much more in keeping, design-wise, with the rest of the Windows 10 interface, although it still opens in a separate window. The Defender Security Center is split into several sections, including antivirus, firewall and device performance.
- Below each of the section icons, you can see basic info about that section, including whether it is currently enabled or not. Click on any of the section titles and you are able to see more information, along with any options available for that particular part of Defender.

Running a Virus Scan

You can scan your PC for viruses in a couple of different ways with Windows Defender. Click the Virus & Threat Protection icon to get started.

1. If you are using a third-party antivirus program, such as Kaspersky or AVG, it will say so at the top of the window. If you want to check exactly which, click the link 'View antivirus providers'. This opens the Windows Control Panel. Click Security to open the panel and look for Virus Protection.

2. You can still use Defender to scan for viruses, with or without other antivirus software present. Back in the Virus & Threat Protection window, click the Quick scan button to get started. A progress bar appears, along with some details of files scanned and time elapsed.

3. You can, if you are not sure the Quick scan is enough, perform an offline scan. This is a much deeper scan and certainly takes longer to perform. It is, however, much more likely to find some of the more devious viruses and other threats. Click Advanced scan and select offline scan > Scan now.

4. The other options here let you check for protection updates, as well as change the Virus & Threat protection settings; for example whether real-time protection is on. You can also choose files or software to exclude from scans and change the notification settings for Windows Defender.

Windows Firewall

A firewall is often the first defence against viruses and other Internet nasties, so make sure you at least use the one provided by Windows 10.

You should always run Windows Firewall even if you have another firewall turned on. Turning off Windows Firewall might make your device, and your network if you have one, more vulnerable to unauthorized access.

To turn Windows Firewall on or off, select the Start button, open Windows Defender Security Center > Firewall & network protection, choose a network profile and then under Windows Firewall, turn it on or off.

Privacy: Make Full Use of the Privacy Tools

Being in control of security on your computer is important but almost as important is being able to control your privacy settings. Microsoft recently launched a web-based privacy dashboard tool and this has now become available to everyone in the Creators update.

The Privacy Dashboard

The privacy dashboard is web-based rather than in the settings and it allows you to manage multiple devices from a single interface, as long as you are logged in to a single account.

1. Open your browser and navigate to www. account.microsoft.com/privacy. If prompted, use your Microsoft account details to log in. You will be logged in to the privacy overview page that lets you quickly see what privacy settings the dashboard contains and controls.
2. Along with the main Search, Browsing and Location privacy categories, if you scroll down to the bottom of the page you will see entries for everything from Apps to Xbox, with simple links to take you to the settings and options for those privacy areas.
3. Click on one of the main categories, Search, Browsing, Location or Cortana, and you will see more information. This could include a list of searches you have made or websites visited (in Edge only, not other browsers), interests Cortana has saved for you or locations you have been.
4. Each section has a Clear button, whether that is clearing browsing history, search history and so on. It is next to a warning that states clearing data will stop Windows being able to provide you with accurate and relevant information. You need to decide what is more important, privacy or recommendations.
5. Another useful privacy section in the dashboard is the Advertising Preferences. This lets you control whether personalised adverts are shown to you in the Edge browser. Some of the ads you may receive on Microsoft websites and apps are tailored to your previous activities and searches.
6. There is also a browser tool that lets you choose if the adverts you see come from companies other than Microsoft. Click the option under

More Choices and wait for the Digital Advertising Alliance scan to finish. You can then choose from the list to see adverts from different advert providers.

Privacy Settings

There are, of course, still privacy options in the main Settings app in Windows 10. This is generally added to and improved with each OS update.

- General Privacy: Privacy has its own section within the settings; here there are many different categories covering everything from Location to Background Apps. Click on each of the privacy categories to see the options within that category. Use the slider switches to allow or block privacy actions.

- Messaging Apps: We're using Windows 10 on a laptop here but if we had a tablet with a SIM card we would be able to get control over which apps were able to send messages over SMS and MMS. You probably want this to be restricted to just your Messaging app; most apps really shouldn't have access to your texts.

- Account Info: Apps are able to access very basic personal settings such as your name and account information. This is so they can sign you in automatically to your Windows account for things like Xbox Live or the Windows Store. You can turn this off wholesale or on an app by app basis.

- Background Apps: You can control which apps you allow to run in the background. If you're on a laptop or desktop this probably won't be that big an issue, but you may want to turn these off on tablet devices to conserve power. Some apps you may not use, like Get Office, really don't need to run in the background.

Social Networks: Secure Yourself on Facebook

Facebook has become one of the best sources for cyber criminals to gain personal information on the Internet. Without realising it, a user is giving out reams of data and in most circumstances they're making it public.

Create a Safer Facebook Profile

The dangers of social media aren't just for young people, many adults have been duped into befriending someone they don't know and exposing their personal information.

1. Facebook's policy forbids the use of fake names but it does allow nick names to be used. Where possible, use your nickname instead of your real name. This will effectively hide your real name details from those who would wish to exploit it.
2. Set up two-factor authentication, alerts about unrecognised logins and make sure that emails from Facebook are encrypted. These can all be found in the Settings > Security and Login section. These three security tools will instantly make Facebook more secure.
3. Go to Settings > Privacy and make sure that the Who can see my stuff section is set for just friends, as opposed to friends of friends or public. This will effectively hide your Timeline contents from others and only your confirmed friends will be able to see any updates.
4. Never post any contact information on your profile. We often automatically start filling in the phone number field on a site but take a moment to consider what the ramifications could be should your number be made aware outside your circle of friends. That also includes house address too.
5. Tempting as it may be, try to avoid posting your location. Whether you're at home alone or you're on holiday, should that information be made available then a criminal will know that your house is empty or worse, that you're alone in it.
6. Try to avoid sharing thoughts of the day, inspirational quotes, fake news or other such items that appear on your Timeline from others. Often these instances are created to farm for shares and likes and can often

be traced back to individuals who are looking for active Facebook accounts.

7. Do not automatically accept every friend request you get. Take a moment to check the person out and if necessary message them to find out who they are and how they know you. If their answer is vague, then it's best to ignore the request, as they could be fishing for information.

8. Not all apps you install on your phone or tablet are good. Take a moment to read what an app will try to access when it's installed. Often a rogue app will attempt to access your Facebook account to farm for information on you and your friends.

9. Whilst in the Settings > Privacy section, consider editing the default options for the Who can look me up fields. These will prevent the public, or even friends of friends, from being able to find you on Facebook, which in turn adds a higher level of security to your account.

10. Finally, ensure that the Do you want search engines outside of Facebook to link to your profile option is set to No. This will hide you from someone who has entered your name into Google in the hope that they might be able to find your Facebook account.

File Backups: Learn How to Protect Your Files

Windows 10 is a very stable and reliable operating system but disaster can still strike on occasion. Being able to create backups of your system and important files is an important skill, one that can save you hours or possibly days of frustration and worry.

Using File History

To back up using File History, you will need a secondary storage drive. This can be an internal or network-connected hard drive or a removable flash drive. We are using a flash drive.

1. The first thing to do is to make sure that your storage drive has enough free space on it. If it is brand new, you don't need to worry about this step but if the drive has been used previously, you should check. Insert the drive into a USB port and open File Explorer.
2. You should see the drive listed with a drive letter, for example: USB Drive (F:). Right-click on the drive name and select Properties from the menu that appears. You can now see how much space is remaining on your flash drive and how much is available in total.
3. Assuming you have a good amount of storage space on the drive, you can begin the process of backing up files. File History backs up copies of files that are in the Documents, Music, Pictures, Videos and Desktop folders and the OneDrive files available offline on your PC.
4. If you have files elsewhere that you want to back up using File History, you'll need to move them to one of these folders before you start to back up. In most cases this can be done using cut and paste (Ctrl + C and Ctrl + V) or by right-clicking the icon of the file and selecting Copy and the same on the folder using Paste.
5. Now open the main Settings app in Windows 10 and click on Update & Security > Backup. Click the 'Add a drive' button and you will hopefully see your USB drive detected. Click on the drive in the list to select it. This is now designated as your backup drive and can be left in the USB port.
6. File History regularly backs up versions of your files in the Documents, Music, Pictures, Videos and Desktop folders and the OneDrive files available offline on your PC. Over time, you will have a complete history

of your files. If the originals are lost, damaged or deleted, you can restore them.

7. Back in the Backup screen of the settings, click on More options. This shows you exactly which folders are backed up and how large the backup is. Your files will not be backed up straight away with File History but you can click the 'Back up now' button to initiate it.

8. You can change how often your computer backs up, from every 10 minutes to once a day. You can also choose how long backups are kept before they are overwritten by new ones. This ranges from one month to forever, although you can also set it so that they are kept until space is needed.

Restoring Backups

It is no good having your files backed up if you don't know how to restore them after a system failure. You will need your storage drive plugged in to your PC to restore files.

1. In the search field of the taskbar, type "restore your files with file history" and click on the result shown. Enter the name of the file you're looking for in the search box or use the left and right arrows to browse through different versions of your folders and files.
2. Select what you want to restore to its original location and then select the Restore button. If you want to restore your files to a different location than the original, press and hold or right-click the Restore button; select Restore To and then choose a new location.

Recovery: How to Create a Recovery Drive

A recovery drive is a useful way to ensure that you don't lose everything on your PC in the event of a critical malfunction. It can help you both troubleshoot and fix problems, even if the PC won't start as it normally would. All you need is a blank, formatted USB flash drive.

Creating the Recovery Drive

Creating a recovery drive is a relatively simple process, although it takes a bit of time, but one which could save a lot of frustration in the future.

1. The first thing you need to do is find a USB drive that is large enough and then make sure it is ready to be used. The USB drive you decide to use won't be able to be used for anything else like storing other files, etc. so make sure it is a spare, or bought specifically for the task.
2. A basic Windows 10 recovery file will be less than 500MB but if you choose to include system files in the backup (recommended), so you can use it to reinstall Windows, you will need much more space. A basic recovery drive can be as small as 1GB but a full recovery drive needs to be at least 8GB.
3. Your USB drive needs to be wiped of everything currently on it before the recovery drive is created. You can do this during the set up process later or you can format it yourself right now: a useful thing to know how to do. Insert your USB drive into a free USB slot on in your computer.
4. Open the File Explorer on your computer and you should see the USB flash drive listed in the sidebar. It will probably be labelled as the (E:) or (F:) drive. Right-click on the drive label and select Format from the action menu. Leave the settings as default (should be FAT32) and then click Start.
5. You should now be ready to create your recovery drive. In the search field, type "Recovery Drive" and select the Create a Recovery Drive result. In newer versions of Windows 10, you might also be able to find the Recovery Drive in the main apps list, opened by clicking the Start menu button.
6. Allow the software to "make changes to this PC" and the setup wizard will open. This first screen is where you choose whether you want to back up system files with the recovery drive, so you can use it to reinstall Windows 10. If you do, tick the checkbox and then click Next.

7. After a few moments, you will be asked to select the USB flash drive you wish to use. If you only have one USB drive inserted, it will be the only one shown and will be automatically selected. You are reminded again how much storage space the drive needs, and that all existing data will be wiped.

8. Click Create on the next screen and the process will begin. This may take a while to complete, so go make a coffee and leave it to run. A progress bar shows how far along it is, should you need to check. Do not remove the USB drive, or turn off your computer, before the process finishes.

9. When the process is complete, you should be prompted to delete the recovery partition on your PC, to save some space; as long as you plan to keep your recovery drive, this is safe to do. If you are not sure, you can leave the recovery partition in place; it can be deleted at a later date if you wish.

10. If you did not already have a recovery partition on your computer, you won't see this step. You will simply be informed that the recovery drive is ready, and to click Finish. Remove the USB drive from your computer and put it somewhere safe. It is a good idea to label the drive so it is not reused.

Windows Store: Explore the Windows 10 Marketplace

Windows 10 comes with great built-in apps including Skype and OneDrive but that's just the beginning. The Store has loads more to help you stay in touch and get things done, plus more games and entertainment than ever before, many of them free!

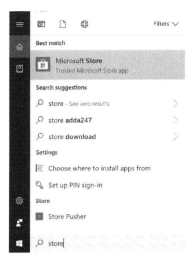

- Category Tabs: Just as with other online app stores, the Windows Store features several different download categories. These include Apps, Games, Music and Films. Each category has its own Home screen, which displays: Most Popular, Top Free and Trending sections.
- Featured Apps: The Featured Apps slider will display those apps or games that are trending or have been particularly popular. This display is constantly updated and is a good way of finding out what other Windows 10 users are using and playing.
- Software Charts: These links take you to lists of the most popular and most downloaded apps and games on the Windows Store. Once you click on one of the links, you can further refine the chart using the links on the left-hand sidebar. Filters include Top Free, Top Paid, Best Rated and New & Rising.
- Apps and Games: As you scroll down the main page of the App, Game, Music or Film Home screens, you will see additional sections showing

Most Popular, Top Free, etc. If you want to see all of the apps in a particular section, click the "Show All" button on the right.

- Downloads/Updates: If there is an update or new download available for any app you currently have installed on your computer, a notification will appear here. The number shows how many updates/app downloads are waiting. Click the arrow and select the required action (update, retry etc.).
- Store Settings: Click the small Account icon here to see the store settings option. Here you will find details of the Microsoft account currently being used, along with several sliders used to control things like automatic app updates. You can also control who can install new apps on your PC.
- Search Bar: You can use the main search bar in the taskbar to search for apps, games, music and films in the Windows Store (store results will have the store icon next to them in the results list). Alternatively, you can search just inside the store by using this search bar.
- Windows Store Offers: Periodically, the Windows Store will feature offers for its users. This could be a free Groove Music 30 day trial, or other download offers. Click on the link to read more about the offer and then follow the instructions to take advantage of it.

Windows Store: Finding Apps and Windows Downloads

There was a Windows Store inside Windows 8 but Microsoft has a new version inside Windows 10. That's because, like the new so-called 'Universal' apps, the Store will work across all Microsoft devices including Windows Phones and the Xbox One.

Take a Look Around

The great thing about the new Windows Store is that the quality of the apps has improved, so it's actually worth browsing. But aside from better apps, the whole experience of looking for new software has been improved in Windows 10.

1. As well as being more responsive to use, the Windows Store has improved vastly in terms of content – as well as apps and games there are now movies to buy or rent and music to download. You can switch between the major sections using the buttons at the top of the window.

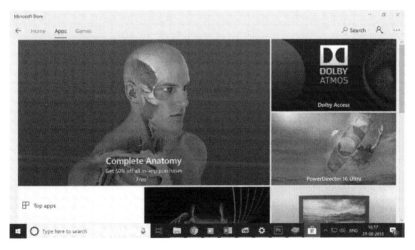

2. Clicking on one of these main sections – here we've clicked on Apps – takes you to a Browse screen where you're presented with the latest apps as well as those that are growing in popularity at the moment. You can also refine your search using the categories on the left – say you just wanted to see Education apps, for example.
3. Each section also features charts of the most downloaded apps as well as curated app recommendations. Here the selection is reasonably

uninspiring but presumably this would improve as you downloaded more apps. You can also easily flick through the top free and paid apps.

4. As in many Windows 10 apps, there's a search box in the top right. The search will pick up results from across the Store, whatever you search for. Here we've found a film we'd like to see. This page is roughly the same whether you're looking at a game, movie or app.

5. You don't to pay for most apps on the Windows Store. There are stacks of apps you can get hold of for free. Each app has a helpful star rating and user reviews, so you can always see which apps aren't ones that are recommended by others.

6. When you download an app or other content, it will be added to your download queue. Apps will download and then install relatively quickly but other content – especially HD movies – could take longer. You can also click the blue Check for Updates button to check for app updates, though these will install automatically.

7. Paid-for apps use your credit or debit card. This is all connected to your Microsoft account and you can view your current account and billing information at account.microsoft.com. You can have multiple payment options should you choose to. At the Microsoft account site you're also able to view what Microsoft services (like Groove Music Pass) you're currently signed up to.

Maps: Explore the Powerful Maps App

Just like Google, Microsoft provides its own Maps app. This incredibly useful tool not only shows you a 2D map of anywhere in the world but also lets you see satellite view, traffic information and even view major cities in 3D. You can even draw or write on top of maps.

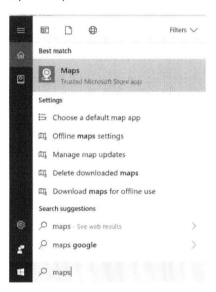

- Directions: You can use the Map app to plan routes: in a car, by public transport and even on foot. Select your chosen transportation method using the icons at the top of the Directions pane. You can either leave the A field as My Location or type a new one. In the B field, type your destination. The route will appear on the map. You can refine the route by clicking the Options button.

- Search: Click the Search button on the left-hand side of the map window and a new pane will open. This pane contains some search suggestions, such as Hotels and Coffee and Shopping, with the standard search field at the top. As you type your search, suggestions will appear in the search pane. You can click any of these to find that location.

- Maps View: The Maps view is the default one for the Maps app. This is what will greet you when you first load the app on your Windows 10 PC. You can zoom in and out of the map using either the + and − buttons on the control panel on the right of the window or by scrolling back and forward with the scroll wheel on your mouse (if you use one).

- Your Location: When you open the Maps app it will try to pinpoint your approximate location. You may be asked to allow this location tracking to happen. Your location will then be show on the map as a small black and grey circle. You can click on this to see more information, if available, and then save the location as a favourite by clicking the star in the pane that opens.
- Windows Ink: Windows Ink allows you to write or draw on a map using the various pen tools (including colours). You can also use the pen to trace a route and have Maps tell you the distance of the line drawn, or even the directions for the route you marked out. You can then save the customised map. It is really very clever and fun to play around with.
- Maps Settings: The Maps app settings let you choose the units of measurement used, depending on your preference and your preferred defaults for directions and location. This last option will be used if the app can't find you, by using location services. You can also download maps for offline use or upload maps that have been saved elsewhere, that have been shared with you perhaps.
- 3D Cities: The 3D Cities button should be fairly self-explanatory. Click the button to open the pane and you will see an alphabetical list of the cities with thumbnails that have been mapped in 3D. Click the Country/Region heading at the top to refine the list. Click on any of the thumbnails to load the 3D map; loading time will vary, depending on your Internet connection speed.
- Saved Places: The Saved Places pane contains all of your saved locations. These can be anything from a favourite coffee shop to the street where you parked your car in a new city. To add places, search for a location and select the star underneath the correct one in the search results list. You then have the option to give the favourite a nickname or set it as Home or Work.
- Rotate & Tilt: The small floating control panel on the right of the Maps window contains several useful tools for changing the current view. The top two controls are rotate and tilt, allowing you to either rotate the map around the central point or tilt the map to give you an isometric view. You can easily centre your view on your location again by clicking the third icon down.

Maps: Learn to Navigate with Maps

Boasting excellent mapping, great aerial photography, up-to-the-minute traffic and the ability to calculate directions by public transport, road or foot, the Maps app is one of the very best ways to navigate. New additions make the Maps app even more useful.

Moving Around in Maps

There are few controls in the Maps app but they allow you to do a lot of things very easily. Let's take a look at how you move around in the app.

- The easiest way to move the map around is to left-click and drag it and use the mouse wheel or trackpad slider to zoom in and out. This allows you to move the map around to focus on the area you need. If you are zoomed far out of the map, double-clicking the mouse zooms in quickly.
- Maps has a dedicated control panel on the side of the window containing, from top to bottom: Rotate, hold pointer on it to see; Tilt, hold pointer over to see options; Show Location; Map Views/Layer; and Zoom in and Zoom out. You can also tilt by holding the right mouse button and moving up and down.
- Clicking on things like Saved Places or 3D Cities in the top control bar, tabs will line up alongside the permanent Search and Directions buttons at the top left of the window. You can then click on them at any time to see the information contained in each pane or tab.
- Right-clicking on the map brings up a small action menu. This lets you set a To location, a From location (for planning a route), add a new destination and drop a pin in a specific location. When you drop a pin, a new window opens allowing you to search for things at that location, add favourites and more.

Planning a Route

Maps is great just for checking out an area, looking around a city or just finding businesses local to you. It is also great for planning detailed routes.

- To start planning a route, click the Directions tab at the top left of the Maps window. A small panel opens with boxes for your starting and ending location. You can either type a destination or you can choose one from the list that appears below the box when you click on it.

- If you need to make detours or multiple stops along your route, you can click the + button to add more destination boxes. Each one can have a destination in it, making up your complete route. When you view directions, each of the destinations you added is marked with a relevant letter.
- Routes vary depending on whether you are driving, walking or need to take public transport. You can quickly flick between these options using the buttons at the top of the directions pane. When you have your start and end points entered and travel method chosen, click Get Directions.
- The route is now shown on the map, with an estimated travel time readout above the destination. If alternative routes are available, they are shown as a light blue line, with the main route shown as a dark blue line. Points along the route are marked, usually where a change of direction is needed.
- If you click Go in the directions pane, Maps switches to a satnav-style view and traces your route as you continue along it. This is more for portable devices such as phones and tablets that you could use for directions in a vehicle. Click the Back button to return to the normal maps view.
- You can also plan a route by drawing it. Click the Ink button and then the Directions tool in the menu that opens. Draw a line along the route you wish to take and Maps refines that into a proper route along roads, missing dead-ends, etc. You can save or share the route just as with any other.

People: Manage Your Contacts in Windows 10

The People app has been a part of Windows 10 for some time but in the more recent update to the OS, it has had an overhaul. New features have been added, along with a brand new taskbar icon. Let's take a look at this excellent way of keeping track of your contacts.

The New People Button

If you can't see the People button in the taskbar, and can't activate it in the action menu, you may be running an older version of Windows 10. Check your available updates.

- After the newest Creators update has installed, you will see a small people icon on the right-hand side of the taskbar. If you don't see the icon (it looks like two people, one standing behind the other), right-click on the taskbar and select "Show the People Button" from the action menu.
- Click on the button and a new People panel will open. Click on the Get started button at the bottom of the new panel. Now click on the Apps tab. This will show you a list of apps that the people app is currently pulling contact information from. It may include apps such as Skype and Mail.
- You may need to connect the apps before People will start checking for contacts. If an app is not already connected, but is available to be, it will have a link next to it: Click to connect this app. The app in question will open and it will be linked to People. Any new contacts in the app will be added.
- The People tab in the panel will eventually show a list of regular contacts, or people you have Shoulder Tapped (or who have Shoulder Tapped you). Right now it will probably be empty and you can't manually add people to this panel; although this option may be added in the future.
- You can open the original (but updated) People app either through the People panel on the taskbar, or by clicking on it in the main apps list in the Start menu. To add a new contact manually to the People app, click on the People button, select the More button and then New Contact.

- The main app will open in a new window and you will be asked to choose and account to save the contact to: usually Outlook but can also include things like Gmail accounts, if you use one. You can then enter the name, phone number and any other contact details in the fields provided.
- You can add a photo to your contacts, just like on a smartphone, if you have one to hand. Click the Add photo circle on the new contact creation screen and navigate to the photo you want to use. The default photo selection is the Photos app but you can browser to any folder you want.
- The new People app allows you to pin a number of contacts to the right side of the taskbar for quick access. Click the People button and then click "Find and pin contacts". A list of your contacts will appear in the panel. Scroll down until you find the contact you want to pin.
- Click on the contact to pin it to the taskbar. A separate window will also open, showing you the contact details. This is the windows that will open each time you click on a pinned contact. A well as the contact details, it also contains links to the main app, and options for unpinning.
- Shoulder Taps are notifications from contacts, from apps like Skype, that animate in the taskbar. To enable Shoulder Taps, go to Settings > Personalisation > Taskbar and scroll down to People. You can enable or disable Shoulder Taps and enable or disable Shoulder Tap sounds here.

Calendar: Explore the Microsoft Calendar App

The Windows 10 Calendar app is a fully integrated planning tool, linked up to your email accounts and can easily be synced to your Windows Phone. Adding new events can be done manually or you can simply use it to view national and public holidays, all of which are automatically added based on your location.

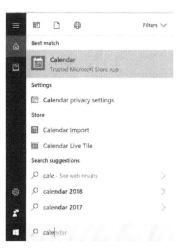

- New Event: There are two main ways to add a new event to your calendar. You can either click on the date in the main window or if the date you want is not in view, you can click the New Event button here. You can then add an event name, location and a start and end date. Give the event a short description, especially if you plan to share it with a contact. You can do that by adding people using the pane on the right of the Add Event screen.

- Month Preview: No matter which view you choose for the main calendar pane - day, week, etc. - the month preview will always show a full month. You can use the arrows above the mini calendar to skip to different months and clicking on a date will then bring that date into view on the main calendar panel. The current day is highlighted in the Month Preview.

- Linked Calendars: Your calendar can be linked to your email account, which will be shown here. If you are using Gmail for your email account, and have any calendars set up in Google Calendar, these will also be shown here. You can use the checkboxes to select and deselect calendars from showing in the main pane and each is colour coded, so you know which custom calendar an event comes from.
- Calendar Pane: The main Calendar pane, however you choose to view it with the view buttons, contains a number of different bits of useful information. Public and national holidays are automatically added based on location. The current day is highlighted in your chosen highlight colour. The current day, along with a few days after, will also show weather and temperature information. Clicking the weather symbol will open the Weather app.
- Calendar View: Along the top of the main window are the controls for changing how the calendar is viewed. The default is the full month view. You can switch to Day or multi-day using the dropdown menu and the calendar will be split into hourly sections. Work Week shows Monday to Friday only, letting you easily plan business or school commitments. To quickly return to the current day, click the Today button here.
- Add Event: Click on any day in the main pane or any hourly slot in day view and a mini Add Event pane will open. You can use this to quickly add an event to your calendar. The pane includes event name, time slots and location; it also lets you choose which custom calendar to add it to. If you want to add more details, click the More Details button. If not, click Done to add the event.
- Calendar Settings: Alongside various customization settings, such as the ability to choose light and dark themes and change the default highlight colour, are settings for adding new email accounts and changing the default view. You can also add public or national holidays manually, in Calendar Settings, if they have not been correctly added automatically. Custom calendar an event comes from.
- Switch to Mail: The Mail and Calendar apps are closely linked and you can quickly switch between the two using the buttons here. Receive an

email with an appointment in it and you can quickly add it to your calendar using the tools in the Mail app. When you switch to the Mail app, it will open in a new window, so the Calendar can be viewed at the same time.

Photos: Learn How to Import Photos in Windows 10

Importing photos from a digital camera or phone on to your PC may seem like a simple task to some but if you have never done it before you can encounter problems and have no idea how to fix them. Let's take a look at importing photos from phone, tablet or camera.

Importing to a Folder

Importing your photos or images directly to a folder on the desktop, or elsewhere, is the traditional method. It tends to be quicker but offers fewer importing options.

1. The first thing you need to do to import photos directly from a phone or camera is to connect the relevant cable to your PC. In almost all cases, this will be a USB cable of some sort. You will have been supplied a transfer cable with the device you are using. Plug this into a free USB port.
2. Plug the other end in to your phone or digital camera and wait a few moments. Your PC should detect the device and may need to install some drivers to make the USB connection work.
3. Normally, when you first plug a device in to your computer which contains storage of some sort, Windows will ask how you want to handle the files in that storage. Scroll down the list to see 'Open in a Folder'. In some cases, Explorer will open showing the connected device.
4. Now click on the device storage: this may be Phone and Card on a smartphone and navigate to where the photos are stored. This will normally be in a folder called DCIM on your phone or camera. You can now simply cut and paste or drag and drop images to a new folder on your PC.

Importing to the Photos App

The Windows 10 Photos app is a great tool for importing photos from a phone, tablet or camera. It allows you to preview and individually pick images more easily, and even sorts them.

1. Open the Photos app on your Windows 10 PC. Now connect your phone or camera to your computer using the relevant USB cable. If you see the popup menu asking how you want to deal with the storage media you just connected, ignore it or click it closed.

2. The Photos app should have opened up with the Collections screen showing. If not, click the tab at the top to open it now. Along the top of the Collections tab are your controls: Refresh, Select, Slideshow and Import. Import is the only one you need to click at this point.

3. The Photos app will now search for photos available to be imported. If your device is not connected properly, or the correct USB drivers are not installed, it will fail to find anything at this point. If you are transferring from a phone or tablet, you may also have to unlock the screen to continue.

4. By default, every image detected on your device will be selected for importing. If you want to import everything, click Continue. If not, you can use the check boxes on the images to select those you want to import; use the Clear All and Select All buttons as required.

5. You can now choose where the imported photos will be saved. By default, this will probably be somewhere like C:\Users\YourName\Pictures. Click the 'Change where they're imported' link to do just that. You can also choose to import into folders arranged by month or day.

6. Click Import. Your image will now begin to appear in the Photos app window, within the Collections section. An album will also be created called Last Import. Click on one of the images shown to begin editing or enhancing it with the tools Photos offers.

Photos: Exploring the Built-in Photos App

You can use the Photos app to view or edit photos and videos in your Pictures library and on OneDrive, and to import photos and videos. The Photos app includes a wide range of editing options to enhance your photos, from automatic fixes to advanced adjustments.

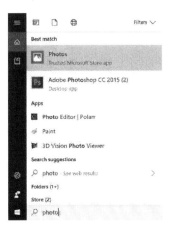

- Search: A new feature to Photos, since the latest update. Search lets you quickly search the name of any photo in your collection, as well as some clever labelling on behalf of Microsoft. Every photo on your system has metadata, which describes its contents. Windows 10 scans the metadata and searches for other contacts, users and even labels such as cat, puppy, fighter jet and so on. Give it a try and see.

- Photos Menu: The new photos app has two main internal sections, Collection and Albums. Alongside these sections are Folders, which show other images on your computer. In the Collection section, you can see a collection of all your photos, grouped by date taken (in reverse chronological order).

- Sort by Date: While in the Collection section, you can quickly find photos from a certain time period without scrolling through all of the ones in the full list. Above each collection you can see a date; click or tap on the date to zoom out to a list of all past months. Click a month to zoom in on that date.

- Photo Collection: All photos within a particular collection are shown here; you can select images by rolling over them with the mouse pointer and checking the boxes that appear in the top corner of each image. Click on any image thumbnail shown on the main screen and it opens in full screen mode.

- Image Editing: Select an image or photo and click on Edit & Create. This will reveal a drop-down menu that allows you to add filters and effects, including hand drawn shapes and images, add stickers and cut outs from Paint 3D and add 3D effects such as rain, confetti and more. There's even an option to make a video with music, using multiple images and photos.

- Photo Albums: The Photos app automatically creates some albums for you, based on images that share characteristics (such as screenshots) but you can also create your own albums. Click the New Album button and all of your images are shown. Select the ones you want to add and click the tick.

- Contextual Menu: With no image selected, the button in the top right corner of the photos app allows you to refresh the view, change to selection mode (for selecting multiple images) or import photos. Once a photo is selected, these buttons change to Share, Copy and Delete image.

- Photos View: These three icons allow you to view the photos in different sizes: large, medium and small. The smaller the photos, the more you can fit on a screen. It's worth experimenting to find the best view that suits you and you can always quickly change the view depending on the folder.

- Full Screen Mode: Once an image in the Photos app is viewed in full screen, you have access to several new tools. Along the top of the image are buttons to Share, create a Slideshow, Enhance, Edit, Rotate and

Delete the image. You can return to the thumbnail view by clicking the Back button.

- Auto Enhance: If you don't want to mess around with image editing, you can try out the Auto Enhance button. Clicking this button once asks the Photo app software to analyse the image and apply changes. This might simply be enhancing the brightness or colour and it could straighten the image as well.

Photos: How to Manage and Edit Your Photos

The Photos app was first introduced in Windows 8 but it wasn't the best experience when compared to most third party apps. In Windows 10 it has been improved, with better ways to browse photos and a lot more editing options to make the most of your images.

Managing Your Images

The Photos app has seen some useful improvements over the last few years and is actually very powerful now. It doesn't offer the flexibility of an app like Photoshop Elements, but it does a lot of simple edits very well.

1. Photos shows all of your images in a scrolling timeline of images, like we're now used to seeing on many smartphones or tablets. This is called your photos Collection. You can click on any image to get a full-window view and then click the Back arrow in the top left corner to return to the main list.

2. Albums is a completely automated feature. If you have an iPhone or iPad, you may have seen Apple's Moments feature; this works in much the same way. Albums gathers together groups of photos you took around the same time, so you can easily look back through them later.

3. If you're signed into Windows 10 with your Microsoft account, you'll also be signed in automatically to the Photos app. The benefit of this is that photos stored on OneDrive also appear in Photos. You can auto-upload photos from the OneDrive app for your phone as you take them.

4. Photos settings, click the More button at the top right, lets you choose whether the Photos app atomically enhances badly exposed photos as well as whether you want the app to show duplicate images as one file; say you saved a photo twice or imported it twice without realising.

5. You can also choose where Photos should look for images here. Your own Pictures folder, plus Windows' public Photos folder are automatically included; but it's really useful to be able to change this if you store your images somewhere else, perhaps an external hard drive you always use.

6. Back to the Photos Collection. You're now going to use the Select feature, found in the menu at the top right. This enables you to select individual or multiple images. You'll see the top menu bar has now

changed, while each image has a tick box appear on it. Click it to choose the images you want.

7. The Photos app allows you to do several things with your photos and images. The first is to email them. Select the images you want to send and click the Share button in the toolbar. The share options window will open, allowing you to choose how to share the images, including Mail.

8. You can also copy your photos and images into another app or File Explorer window. To do this, select the photos you want, then click the Copy button in the toolbar (the old Ctrl-C keyboard shortcut works too). You can then paste the photos wherever you want on your computer.

9. To delete photos, select them as detailed previously and click the Delete button in the Toolbar. You will see a pop-up to confirm you want to continue with the action. Deleted photos are moved to the recycle bin anyway, so you have a chance to retrieve photos deleted in error.

10. The final tool in the Select toolbar is the Add to Album button. This adds any images you have selected to either one of the auto-created albums, or to an album you create for the purpose. Click 'Create new album' in the popup window, give it a name and then click 'Create album'.

Drawing on Images

The Photos app in Windows 10 allows you to draw or write on top of your images, as long as you have installed the Anniversary update, and then save them as a completely new file.

1. Open the Photos app and select your image (or double click an image to open it in Photos if that is the default app). Along the top of the image are several buttons, click the Draw button to begin editing your image. You will see a new set of buttons and controls appear at the top.

2. From left to right, these buttons allow you to draw/write in pen style, pencil style, calligraphy style, erase, switch out of touch writing mode, save your file, share your file, and exit drawing mode. If you click on any button and see a small arrow, click again to open a contextual menu for it.

3. The contextual menus allow you to change the colour and the thickness of the pen or pencil tools. When you have picked a style, colour and size, you can begin to draw or write over the top of your image. The drawing tool in Photos works best with a touchscreen PC, of course.

4. Once you have completed drawing or writing on your image, you can save it. If you want to retain the original image, change the name of the edited image in the save dialogue box before you finish. If you click on Share, a list of sharing possibilities will appear to choose from.

Editing Images

The image editing tools in the Photos app have been improved and added to in the Anniversary update, including the addition of preset filters and effects.

1. Open your image in Photos and click on the Edit button at the top right of the screen. If you had the Photos app running in full screen, the image will be shrunk down slightly to fit the new toolbar, down the right of the of the editing window.

2. Starting at the top of the editing toolbar, you have the crop and rotate button. Click this to see further options for managing the aspect of your image. You can choose a preset aspect ratio, or drag the handles at the corners to crop to a custom shape.

3. If you need to straighten the image, you can do so using the handle to the right of the photo. Click on this and move your mouse up or down to carefully rotate the image in small amounts. As you do this, a grid appears to help you line up the photo. Click Finished when done.

4. Moving down the main edit toolbar you will see the Enhance button. You can click this to let the software make changes and improvements to the image automatically. You will see the image change slightly, and you can then use the slider on the button to increase or decrease those changes.

5. You can, of course, apply enhancements yourself. Below the auto-enhance button are the photo filters. Click on any of these to see the changes applied to your image. You can apply a filter and then adjust its effects by clicking on the Adjust tab at the top of the toolbar.

6. The tools in the Adjust tab allow you to tweak the Light, Colour, Warmth and Clarity of an image. You can also use a slider to apply a Vignette (lighten or darken the edges of an image). Just use the sliders to adjust any of these effects until you are happy with your image.

7. At the bottom of the Adjust tab are Spot Fix and Red Eye tools. Click Spot Fix and the cursor will change to a blue circle. Place this over the part of the image you want to fix and click. The software will try to match the location of dot to the scenery or colour around it, hopefully removing it.

8. The Red Eye tool works in a similar way. Click the tool and move the circle cursor over the red part of your subject's eye and zoom in if you

need to. The tool will try to take the red out of the image and match it to the surrounding colour. The results are usually very good.

Spotify Music: Listening to Music with Spotify

Recently, Microsoft announced that Groove music would be completely replaced by Spotify in Windows 10. Spotify is an extremely good music playback and discovery app, so this is definitely a good move. Let's take a look at using Spotify in Windows 10.

Exploring the Spotify App

The free version of Spotify offers a great selection of features and access to loads of music. However, if you want an ad-free experience, you will need to buy a premium account.

1. You can download and install the Spotify app from the Windows store for free. It is also free to use, although some of the features will need a premium (paid) account. Once downloaded and installed, you can either create a Spotify account to sign in or you can sign in with Facebook.
2. If you have used Groove Music before, the layout and controls of Spotify should be fairly familiar. The main areas of the app (music store, radio, local files, etc.) are accessed by using the menu on the left-hand side of the main window. The playback controls are always along the bottom.
3. When you first open the app, the browse screen will be displayed. Here you can see new releases, charts, albums, podcasts and other media to stream and buy. A premium account will allow you to listen to almost everything you see here, and elsewhere within Spotify.
4. Click the radio link in the left sidebar and you can see a selection of digital radio stations to listen to. These will be a random selection of music by different artists and different genres. Just roll your mouse over a radio station and click the play button to start listening.
5. When you use the app more, it will learn the types of music you like to listen to and display more of that type (or similar) on the radio screen. You can also create your own radio station by clicking the Create button at the top and searching for artists or genres you like.
6. Music you have downloaded or bought, and any music stored on your computer, will appear under the Your Library heading in the left sidebar. You can view all of this music by song, album, artist, recently played, etc. Clicking Local Files will display only those songs actually stored on your PC.

7. To play any individual song in your library, simply find it in one of the lists, move the mouse pointer over the song title and click the play button that appears. You can also select the song and then use the playback control panel at the bottom of the Spotify window (this is always displayed).

8. If you are browsing albums, you can click the green play button at the top of the list of tracks. This will begin playing all music in the album, or within the folder that is being viewed. Right-click on any song title and you will see more options, such as viewing other songs from that artist, or opening a radio.

9. You can create your own playlists in Spotify, containing any selection of songs you want. Click New Playlist in the menu on the left, give your playlist a name and click Create. It will then be displayed in your library and will also open within the main window, prompting you to add music.

10. To add songs to your playlists, find a song in your library and right-click on it. From the action menu that appears, click Add to Playlist and then select the playlist you want to add it to. If you have Spotify on your phone or tablet, your created playlists will show up there as well.

Skype: Exploring the Skype App

Skype is a great way of keeping in contact with friends and family in faraway places, without running up huge phone bills. It allows you to phone, video chat and instant message, all from within the same easy-to-use interface. It can even be installed on a mobile device so you never miss a Skype call whilst away from your PC.

- Skype Controls: Most of the Skype controls are now arranged along the left-hand edge. From top to bottom: Recent conversations, Contacts, Bots, Help, Settings and Account info. The default view should normally be the Recent conversations panel and the default theme is the dark one shown here. You can change this by clicking the Settings button at the bottom.

- Bots: Bots are artificially intelligent programs that can do many useful things like search for news, summarise webpages, play games and more. You can start chatting with a bot just like you chat with friends. For example, add the Bing News bot and start a conversation. Type a word such as "finances" and the bot will return news stories into the feed.

- Call/Message Log: You will see all of your recent calls and messages listed here, both in and out. Click on any of the logs to see the conversation or details about the call. The log is split up into days, with a larger Older then a week section at the bottom of the list. At the top is a search bar, allowing you to search for contacts or specific conversations.

- Call Controls: If a contact (or conversation with a contact) who uses Skype is selected, you will see the call controls in the top right corner. This may only be a voice-call button or it may also show a video-call button. The third icon is a group call button, allowing you to add contacts to a group call or message.

- Main Video/Chat Panel: This is where the video will appear when you start a video call with Skype, or where the chat conversation will be displayed if instant messaging. If no conversations are selected in the recent panel, it will display your avatar (the image you use for your account) and a prompt to start a conversation. Clicking this opens your contacts list.

- Dialler Keypad: Clicking this button (or pressing Ctrl + D) will open the dialler on the right-hand side of the screen and allow you to enter a phone number to call. If you are making calls to non-skype contacts, you will need to have Skype credit in your account. If you need to add credit, click the Add credit link and follow the instructions.
- Instant Message: In addition to being able to make calls, Skype also allows you to send instant messages, just like in apps like MSN and Facebook chat. Click inside the text field and type your message to the contact that is currently selected. You can add emoticons to a message by clicking the smiley face at the end of the text field. Click Send to send your message. If the contact is offline, they will receive the message the next time they log in to Skype.

Skype: Making Calls with the Skype App

Now that Microsoft owns Skype, it has incorporated it into Windows 10. Skype keeps the world talking. Say 'hello' with an instant message, voice or video call; and all for free, whichever device you use Skype on. Moreover, it's available on phones, tablets, PCs and Macs.

Install and Use Skype

Recently updated, Skype has now been turned into a proper Windows 10 app and follows the Windows design style more closely.

1. Skype has a dedicated Windows 10 app and this may be preinstalled on your Windows PC but you might need to download it from the Windows store. You can also download Skype directly from http://www.skype.com www.skype.com as well as check that you have the latest version available.
2. Once installed, you will need to sign in to the Skype app. If you already have a Skype account, which is completely free to set up, just enter your login details when prompted. If not, you can go to www.login.skype.com and create a new account in just a few minutes.
3. The Skype window should now be open on screen. The default view is the Recent conversations screen but this may be completely empty if you are new to Skype. The first thing you need to do as a fresh user, is to begin adding contacts.
4. Click the Contacts button (2nd button down from the top) and either select the add contact icon at the bottom of the sidebar or click directly in the search text box and type the name, Skype name or email of the person you want to add. Click Search Skype.
5. Select your friend from the search results, assuming you can see them in the list, and click Add to Contacts. Type a quick note to introduce yourself and then click Send. They will receive a request from you, along with the message and can choose whether to accept you or not.
6. You can select any contact from your contacts list and then either instant message them or start a voice or video call. If the contact you click on has Skype, the call option buttons will appear in the top right corner of the window. Click the relevant button to start a call.
7. Skype instant messaging makes it easy to keep in touch with your contacts and groups wherever they are. You can share files, photos and

contacts. To instant message one of your contacts, select their name and start typing at the bottom of the main window.

8. If you want to make calls to contacts not using Skype (you can make calls to mobiles and landlines too), you will need to add some Skype credit. To do this, click on your profile picture in the bottom left and click the 'Add Skype credit' link.

9. Skype also now includes Bots. Bots are artificially intelligent programs that can do many useful things like search for news, summarise webpages, play games and more. You can start chatting with a bot just like you chat with friends, just choose a bot and click Get started.

10. Bots vary in how useful they are but some are well worth taking a look at. Take the Bing News bot for example. Add this and then type a word ("Crime" for example) in the conversation window. The bot will return news stories based on that subject.

OneDrive: Using the New Files On-Demand Tools

With Files On-Demand, you can access all your files in the cloud without having to download them and use storage space on your device. All your files, even online-only files, can be seen in File Explorer and work just like every other file on your device.

Using Files On-Demand

Files On-Demand allows you to access your storage in a much easier and more efficient way, treating cloud-based files as if they are on your PC.

1. First, make sure you are signed in to OneDrive on your computer. Right-click the white OneDrive cloud icon in the notification area, at the far right of the taskbar. If you don't see the OneDrive icon on the taskbar, click the 'Show hidden icons' arrow, also at the bottom right of the screen.

2. You should see a panel pop-up asking if you want to turn on Files On-Demand. If so, click the blue button and wait whilst OneDrive sets this up. If you don't see this panel, click Settings from the OneDrive action menu, click the Settings tab and then check 'Save space and download files...'.

3. You can now open your OneDrive folder to begin checking how your files are currently stored, and to change the status of any you want to move offline or online. You will see the files and folders on OneDrive now have symbols attached to them, showing you their current status.

4. To mark a file or folder for offline use or as online-only, right-click on it and look in the action menu for 'Always keep on this device' or 'Free up space' depending on what you wish to do. If you mark a folder as 'Always keep on this device', new files in that folder are set as always available files.

5. Sometimes you might want to make sure a folder doesn't show up on a device for privacy reasons. In the OneDrive Activity Center, select the Settings gear. Next to the location where you want to choose folders, click Choose folders. Clear the check box next to the folder you want to keep off this device.

6. When you delete an online-only file from your device, you delete it from your OneDrive on all devices and online. You can restore deleted files and folders from your OneDrive recycle bin on the web for up to 30 days. If you delete a locally available file, it also appears in your device recycle bin.

On-Demand Files

Once the Files On-Demand is set up, you can access everything from within the File Explorer in Windows 10. You can also access them through the OneDrive taskbar icon.

- Viewing Files: When you turn on Files On-Demand, you see all your files in File Explorer and get new information about each file. New files created online or on another device appear as online-only files, which don't take up space on your device. When you're connected to the Internet, you'll be able to use the files like every other file on your device.
- Online-only Files: Online-only files don't take up space on your computer. You see a cloud icon for each online-only file in File Explorer but the file doesn't download to your device until you open it. You can only open online-only files when your device is connected to the Internet.
- Locally Available Files: When you open an online-only file, it downloads to your device and becomes a locally available file. You can open a locally available file anytime, even without Internet access. If you need more space, you can change the file back to online-only.
- Always Available Files: Only files that you mark as 'Always keep on this device' have the green circle with the white check mark. These files will always be available even when you're offline. They are downloaded to your device and take up space.

Facebook: Using the Facebook App in Windows 10

Like it or not, Facebook has changed the way we communicate through social media. Since the company's launch in 2004, the platform has had its fair share of positive and negative media. With over 2.2 billion monthly active users, Facebook is here to stay.

Be Connected. Be Discovered.

If you prefer not to visit Facebook via your browser, the Windows Store has a specially developed app for both PC and mobile platforms that's just as functional as the web-based interface.

1. First, open the Windows 10 Store. In the Search box, located in the top right of the Store window, type Facebook. The first option available, labelled App, is what you're looking for. Simply click it to be taken to the Facebook app page in the Store.
2. The Store front details the specifics regarding the app you're currently viewing, Facebook in this instance. Scroll down through the app's page to view a description, any updated information, system requirements, additional information and what functionality the app uses, in case you're concerned over privacy and such.
3. Scroll back to the top of the Facebook app page in the Store. To install the app on to your PC, simply click the blue-coloured Install button. This will initiate the download and installation process. The Facebook app weighs in at around 140MB, which isn't too hefty for a modern app.
4. Once the installation process is complete, you receive a brief notification in the bottom right of your Windows desktop. There are two options available from the notification, Launch and Pin to Start. While you can Launch the app right away, we recommend clicking Pin to Start. This will place the app in the available Groups from the Start button.
5. Click the Start button. If you decided to Pin to Start, as in the previous step, you can now see that Facebook is available as a tile within the Groups section. This allows you to right-click the tile and opt to resize, turn off live tiles, move, unpin from start and so on.

6. Naturally, the next step of the process is to single left-click the Facebook tile to launch it. When launched, the app requests your Facebook user details to log in; enter them into the boxes provided and click the Log in button. If you don't currently have a Facebook account, click on the Sign up for Facebook link.

7. Clicking the Sign up for Facebook link will open your default browser to the Facebook Create an Account page. Enter your details and take a moment to view the company's current Terms and Conditions, along with the Data Policy. When your account has been set up, you can close the browser and return to log in at the app.

8. If you don't already have the Location feature enabled within Windows 10, you will receive a notice when you log into Facebook via the app. It's up to you if you want to enable this feature. Clicking OK will remove the notification but leave the Location setting in Windows 10 unchanged.

9. If you want to enable Location for Facebook, click on the Start button and enter Location into the search. Click on the Location Privacy Settings result and then enable the Location feature and even specify which apps have access to your precise location.

10. The Facebook app presents a slightly more compact view than that of the web-based version. Current online friends are listed down the right-hand side of the screen, while your News Feed and groups are listed down the left. There's the search bar along the top, with friend requests, messages, notifications and your profile settings.

WhatsApp: Using WhatsApp in Windows 10

At its heart, WhatsApp is simply a free to use cross-platform instant messaging service but to its many users the app is much more than just a means of keeping in touch. In just nine years, WhatsApp has grown into one of the most used messaging apps available.

Set Up and Use WhatsApp

With an audience of over 1.3 billion and growing, WhatsApp shows no sign of slowing down. Here's how to install and use it via the Windows Store.

1. You need to install WhatsApp and create an account on your phone before you can use it. The app has been developed for Android, iOS and Windows Phone. Tap the Store icon on your phone, searching for WhatsApp. Tap the correct search and you're taken to the relevant page on the Store.

2. With the WhatsApp page on the Play Store open, tap on the Install button and the process with begin. Some phones already have a version of WhatsApp preinstalled by the manufacturer. You can see if yours is one such device as it displays Update and Open buttons. From here it's recommended to tap Update.

3. Once the update or install has finished you will be left with an Open button and Uninstall if you prefer to remove it; you may not be able to remove a preinstalled version though. Tap Open to launch WhatsApp. Now follow the on-screen instructions to begin the set up of WhatsApp, using the phone's number to pair the app with the device.

4. Once you've installed WhatsApp and set up an account on your phone, you can turn your attention to the Windows 10 app. Open the Windows Store and search for WhatsApp Desktop. When the app's page loads up, click the Get button (if your PC doesn't already have it) to begin the installation.

5. When the installation is complete, click on the Pin to Start option within the notification that pops up. WhatsApp can now be located by clicking on the Start button, it's in the groups section, and right-clicking lets you move, resize and unpin the app accordingly.

6. Click the app's tile to open WhatsApp. The app window opens with a generated QR Code, which can be scanned in by WhatsApp on your

phone. This process matches the account and automatically logs you into your own WhatsApp profile.

7. You need to open WhatsApp on your phone, then tap on the three vertical dots in the upper right, followed by WhatsApp Web. Point the device's camera at the QR Code and the autologin process will start. If the QR code isn't recognised, you may need to wait a moment for a new QR Code to be generated.

8. The autologin feature takes a few seconds and you may get a notification on your phone indicating a successful login from your Windows 10 PC. With the WhatsApp window open, you can browse through your chats using the left-hand pane, while the chat contents are displayed in the right pane.

9. There are numerous options along the top of the app. The three horizontal dots represent further settings that can be applied either to a chat, user or your own profile. The icon in the top left of the WhatsApp window is your own profile and from there you can upload a new profile image and edit your personal visibility in WhatsApp.

10. WhatsApp on the Windows 10 desktop provides limited functionality compared to what's available in the mobile version. However, you can still create new chats and groups and update your status as you would when using the app on your phone.

Netflix: Watching Movies with Netflix

Netflix is something most of us take for granted these days but did you know that it was founded over twenty years ago? The content streaming side of the company started in 2007 and since then its audience has grown to a staggering 120 million users.

Binge Watching

With an ever growing number of shows and movies available, it's hard not to end up binging on Netflix for hours at a time. Here's how to install it from the Windows 10 Store.

1. Start by opening the Windows 10 Store. In the search box type Netflix, to bring up the list of available apps. The Netflix app is the first option available. Click it to view the app's page in the Store.
2. It's worth taking a moment to scroll through the page and view the system requirements, additional information and especially the company's privacy, terms and conditions and licensing terms.
3. Depending on your Windows 10 setup, you may find you already have the Netflix app preinstalled on your system. It depends on how and who set the system up in the first place. If you already have Netflix you can skip these next couple of steps. Otherwise, click the Install button at the top of the window.
4. When the installation is complete a notification pops up in the bottom right of your desktop. Of the two options available within the notification, choose Pin to Start to put the app in the groups section in the Start menu.
5. With the Netflix tile in the group section, you can right-click it to move, resize, turn Live Tiles on or off, unpin or even uninstall it. When you've applied any changes you want to the tile, click it to launch Netflix.
6. If you already have a Netflix account, click the Sign In button in the top right of the app's window. Otherwise, you can opt to join free for a month by clicking on the relevant button in the middle of the window.
7. Clicking on the Join Free button takes through the process of creating a new Netflix account. There are currently three options available, detailing what you get for the monthly fee, and more importantly, how much it costs. You need to enter your credit or debit card details but you can cancel at any time.

8. Netflix now offers full High Dynamic Range (HDR) streaming on the Windows 10 app. However, you need a really good PC in order to be able to enjoy 4K content. The minimum spec requires you to have a 7th generation CPU or higher, 8GB of main RAM and an Nvidia 1050 GPU with 3GB of memory, or the AMD equivalent.

9. You can use the search bar to look for specific movies and shows within Netflix or browse through the Popular section to see if anything fits the bill. Note, the more shows and movies you watch, the more your Top Picks choices will be populated.

10. Netflix have introduced an offline function whereby you can download content to watch later, thus saving on bandwidth and eliminating any buffering issues at certain times of the evening. All you need to do is look for the Download & Go icon, then go to My Downloads to view your offline content.

Night Light: Discover the Night Reading Mode

Most screens give off blue light, which is known to activate our brains and keep us awake. It can also cause tired eyes. The latest version of Windows 10 (Creators Update) has added a Night Light mode to the settings. This will take much of the blue light out of the monitor.

Set Up and Use Night Light

There are a couple of different ways you can use Night Light mode and a few settings that can be used to make it perfect for your display and personal preference.

1. To turn Night Light on, head in to Settings > System > Display. At the top of the display settings you will see the Night Light slider switch and you can simply click the slider to turn Night Light on as you need it. If you don't see it, you will need to check that you have updated Windows 10 with the Creators update.

2. As soon as you click the slider you see the screen change. Some of the blue light is stripped out and the colour shifts towards the red spectrum. If you don't see a change, it may be that the feature is configured to activate during certain set hours (between 19:00 and 7:00, for example).

3. Click Night Light Settings and then Turn on now, if you just want the feature activated. Alternatively, you can set a schedule, so that your device switches to Night Light mode at the same time each evening. Click 'Schedule night light' and choose the on and off times using the clock interface.

4. You can also alter the colour temperature of the display change when Night Light is activated. Some displays may respond better to the default change than others, so if you think you need more blue light blocked out (or less), use the colour slider to change the amount until it suits you.

Storage Sense: Using the Storage Management Tools

When your Windows 10 computer begins to run out of space, typically you use different tools, such as Disk Clean-up. You can now use Storage Sense to automatically get rid of junk files. In this guide, we'll show you the steps for setting up this feature.

Updated Storage Sense

Storage Sense has been a part of Windows 10 for some time but it has been updated and added to in the Creators update. If you don't see the options mentioned here, make sure your OS is up-to-date.

1. To enable Storage Sense on Windows 10, open Settings > System > Storage. Click on the Storage Sense toggle switch. Once you enable the option, Windows 10 will automatically delete junk files from your PC, including some temporary files and items in the recycle bin older than 30 days.
2. Storage Sense isn't a manual storage wipe. If you need to clear out space right now, and you have large files in the recycle bin that aren't 30 days old, you will need to delete them manually. Things like old versions of Windows, installation files and update logs will also need to be removed manually.
3. You can, within certain limitations, select which items Storage Sense should remove automatically. In Settings > System > Storage, click on the 'Change how we free up space' link below the Storage Sense slider. You can see that there are three different options, which can be combined in any way you like.
4. You can also see the option to 'Delete previous versions of Windows'. These are deleted anyway, but not for several days after an update. If you really need to clear some space, select the option and then just click the Clean Now button and wait for the process to complete.

Bloatware: Learn How to Remove Unwanted Apps

Giving free upgrades to Windows 10 for existing Windows users was an almost inevitable step by Microsoft but this has seen an increase in bloatware, similar to that seen on Android devices. Thankfully there are ways to remove or disable most of it.

Working with 10AppsManager

Adding software to remove other software may seem counterintuitive but this is a safer way to clean up bloatware than trying to remove it manually.

1. You can download the 10AppsManager software from a variety of file download sites or you can get it directly from the creators at The Windows Club (www.thewindowsclub.com). It should be free wherever you download it from, so don't be fooled into paying for this software.
2. Extract the contents of the downloaded 10AppsManager zip file and place the folder in your Program Folder and pin the shortcut of its .exe file to your Start menu. Do not separate out the contents of the Program folder. You don't need to install the software.
3. As when making any large system changes to your computer, you should create a system restore point first. You can do this via Start menu > Control Panel > System Properties > System Protection. Configure the restore settings and click "Create".
4. You can now double-click the 10AppsManager .exe file to open the software on your computer. The extremely simple main interface will now open. Each of the tiles represents a piece of preinstalled software that you can uninstall if you have no use for it.
5. Click on any of the tiles and then confirm that you want to uninstall the app. You may need to wait a few seconds for the process to complete. You can delete as many preinstalled apps as you wish but if an app does not appear as a tile on the screen, you won't be able to add it.
6. You can reinstall any of the apps you uninstall through 10AppsManager. The only slight annoyance is that the software doesn't remove or alter the tile once the app is uninstalled, so it is a good idea to make a note of which apps you remove from your system.

Disabling Other Features

There are several other features that, although not technically bloatware, might not be doing your computer performance any favours. Let's take a look at some of the worst offenders.

1. Targeted Ads: Windows 10 assigns every user a unique advertising ID to make it easier to provide you with targeted adverts. While this cannot be removed, it can be disabled. Head to the "General" tab in the Windows 10 Privacy menu. Disable the topmost toggle switch labelled "Let apps use my advertising ID ...".

2. Getting to Know You: Meant to streamline the new Windows 10 user experience, the Getting to Know You feature records logs of your typing history, saves recordings of your voice, collects information from your contacts etc. Go to Start menu > Settings > Privacy > Speech, linking & typing > Stop Getting to Know Me.

3. App Location Access: Windows 10 third-party apps can access your location, webcam, microphone and more by default. Not all apps require these permissions. Go to Start menu > Settings > Privacy > Location and remove those permissions that seem unnecessary. Repeat for things like camera and microphone.

4. Background Apps: This last option seems simple but it can make a big impact in terms of battery life and performance. From the Privacy menu, scroll down to the bottom of the menu, then select the "Background apps" option. From here, simply use the toggle switches to prevent these apps from running on start-up.

Maintenance: Using the Built-in Maintenance Tools

Before you start to add software to help with maintenance, it is worth checking out the numerous tools included with the OS. These are spread out over several menus but once you find them you will see that they can really help with security and performance.

Maintaining Windows 10

Windows 10 is a lot better at keeping you informed of problems than previous versions were. It is, however, up to you to keep on top on maintaining the OS if you want the best experience.

Storage Sense: Activating Storage Sense lets the system software automatically free up storage space by getting rid of files you no longer need. These can include temporary files such as cookies and the contents of your Recycle Bin.

You can choose when files are deleted, e.g. after 30 days in the Recycle Bin or if apps don't use them for a certain amount of time. Alternatively you can simply click a button to Clean Now rather than setting automatic cleaning. You can find the Storage Sense option in Settings > System > Storage.

Background Apps: One of the easiest ways to conserve power (for laptop users) and reduce processor strain, is to take control of Background Apps. These are apps that are, by default, allowed to receive info, send notifications and update in the background.

Background Apps You can either stop all background apps with a single slider click or you can prevent individual apps from running in the background.Go to Settings > Privacy > Background Apps and look through the apps listed. If you see apps that you don't need notifications or updates from, click the slider to disable its background activity.

Troubleshooters: Windows 10 includes a number of troubleshooting tools, aimed specifically at certain problems such as audio loss or patchy Internet connection. This is often the best place to start when trying to solve problems with your PC and Windows 10, as the OS contains many drivers for common devices and may just need a small software update.

You simply look through the list of troubleshooters and click on the one which applies. Choose Run the Troubleshooter and then follow the instructions to try and solve the problem. You can find the troubleshooters in Settings > Update & Security > Troubleshoot.

Disk Management: The Disk Management tool is more about diagnostics than actual maintenance but it is a useful way of checking whether your hard disk has space available and is healthy. The panel will show all of your disks, as well as all of the partitions.

Disk Tools: There are several tools built in to Windows 10 (and also in older versions of the OS) that allow you to clean, fix and manage your hard disk. Open the File Explorer and look in the left-hand column for 'This PC'. Select it and then right-click on Local Disk (C:). In the General tab, you will see a button for Disk Clean-up that lets you get rid of temporary Internet files, old program files and so on.

If you click the Tools tab, you can use the Error Checking tool and the Disk Defragment tool. Both of these tools can help your hard disk run more efficiently. Click on either button and follow the instructions for each.

Each column contains information about capacity, free space in MB, percentage of free space and health status. There are some further options, such as the ability to change drive letters and mark partitions as active but they are probably not worth playing around with unless you know what you are doing.

Task Manager: Learn How to Manage Apps and More

The Task Manager is a very useful tool but even if you have been using Windows for some time, you might never have looked at it before. The Task Manager contains information on PC performance, the number of running apps, how many processes are pulling power from the processor and much more. To open task manager, right click on the taskbar and then click "Task Manager". Once open, click on "More details" at the bottom left of the window.

- Processes Tab: The Processes tab is the default tab when the Task Manager is opened. You can open the task manager by simply searching for it in the main search panel. Just as with any other app or piece of software in Windows 10, you can pin a shortcut to the Task Manager, to the taskbar or as a desktop icon.
- Process List: With the Processes tab selected, a list of all processes is shown. Processes are bits of software that run in the background, either running or waiting to run when a corresponding action is taken. As you can see from the list here, things like Cortana and AVG are shown; these you would obviously want to leave.
- Resource Usage: If you find your PC becoming slow and sluggish during normal use, you may have too many processes running. By looking at the resource usage chart, you can see exactly which apps are taking up the most processing power, physical memory, disk space and even network bandwidth. If something is particularly resource hungry, you can right-click and stop it.
- Start-up Tab: The Start-up tab contains a list of all the apps, programs and processes that are enabled every time you start your computer. If

your computer is brand new, this list should be fairly small and filled with essential items. But as you install new apps and software, this start-up list can become bloated and slow down boot up. You can disable auto start-up here.

- Performance Tab: Another useful tab in the Task Manager is Performance. This gives you a real-time performance overview, allowing you to pinpoint exactly how well your hardware is coping with whatever you are doing at the time. If Task Manager is the only app open, the performance chart should be very stable but if you are running several apps, it will show any power spikes.

- Fewer Details: You can view a limited version of the Task Manager by clicking on the "Fewer Details" button at the bottom of the window. This makes the window small enough that it can be left open, in the corner of your desktop for example, but still show relevant information. You can get more information at any time by clicking "More Details".

Updates: What to Keep Updated in Windows 10

Discussing updates is one thing but how do you go about making sure that you have the latest updates and that all the necessary components are being updated correctly? Thanks to the improved update process of Windows 10, this is surprisingly easy.

Keeping Up-to-date

Whilst it's easy to update Windows 10, there are elements that can be missed. We've already mentioned that it's not only Windows that needs updating but also software and drivers.

1. The first port of call is undoubtedly Windows Update. Click on the Windows Start button followed by Settings, the cog icon just above the power icon on the strip to the side. This will open the Windows Settings interface; locate the last entry, Update & Security and click it.
2. By default, Windows Update will automatically check for, download and install updates for the core Windows 10 files. You can check for any on the spot by clicking the Check for updates button and you can see what's already been updated by clicking the Update history link, under the update button.
3. If you click on the Advanced Options link under the Update Settings section, you can then tick a box that enables Windows to automatically check for updates for other Microsoft products, such as Office. It's recommended to make sure the box is ticked, for better security and protection.
4. Within the Advanced Options page click the link for Choose how updates are delivered. This page details the way Windows updates can be pushed to other computers on your network, or even the Internet. Whilst it's a grand idea, there are concerns over privacy from some factors of the community. It's your choice but we prefer this option Off.
5. Hardware drivers are usually automatically updated by Windows Update but whilst signed by Microsoft the drivers themselves aren't always the latest versions. Therein lies a problem: even though signed, the MS drivers won't utilise the hardware as well as the driver developed by the hardware manufacturer.

6. In such cases it's often best to use the hardware manufacturer's driver, as this is more up-to-date and features security patches as well as performance updates. For example, if you own an Nvidia graphics card right-click the Nvidia icon in the taskbar and select Open Nvidia GeForce Experience.

7. The Nvidia GeForce Experience allows you to improve in-game graphics and check for the latest drivers. Usually this is done automatically and you are notified of any available drivers. However, If you want to check manually, click on the Drivers tab followed by Check for Updates.

8. Third-party programs and applications also require regular update checks. Again, this is usually done automatically; when you launch the program in question it often checks for the latest version. If not, look for links such as Check for Updates or similar, usually in the Help, About or even under the File menus of your favourite app.

9. If you've attached some hardware and Windows 10 hasn't been able to load a driver for it, and there isn't any documentation detailing the driver (this often happens with hardware purchased from eBay etc.), then you'll need to hunt one down. Start by locating the device's product name and number and entering it into a search engine.

10. You can often force Windows 10 to locate a driver by right-clicking the Windows Start button and choosing Device Manager from the menu. In the Device Manager window, select the hardware you want updating, right-click it and select Update Driver.

Disk Clean-up: Free Up Storage Space in Windows 10

Disk Clean-up is the best way to free up space on your PC. It will clear up redundant files accumulating on your hard drive including temporary files and Downloaded Program files; but that's not the only way you can free up space, as you'll see.

Clearing Space on Your PC

It's worth giving your machine a little spring clean every so of en to keep it lean. And that doesn't just mean removing unwanted files and folders from the desktop. Disk Clean-up should be an essential part of your PC maintenance.

1. Clean Up: Disk Clean-up is a utility included with every copy of Windows. When you launch it (search for it using the search box on the taskbar), you'll get this small window appear. It will help you rid your PC of detritus that builds up over time as you download files from the Internet or install and uninstall apps.
2. Which Drive?: You'll be asked to select the drive you want to clean up. Most of the time there'll only be one drive you wish to clean up (your C: drive), but it could well be that you've got more than one storage drive on your PC. Disk Clean-up will then begin to scan your drive for things it can sweep up.
3. Scan Results: If you're scanning a second hard drive, it's unlikely Disk Clean-up will find a lot on it as it is mostly concerned with Windows files. And that's what we're looking at here in the results window. As you can see, you can check which items you want to remove from your PC. Click OK to remove.
4. System Files: We actually didn't click OK in the last step; instead clicking the Clean Up System Files option. This won't harm your Windows installation, but will clean up extraneous files that some people prefer to keep. If you upgraded from an old copy of Windows, this includes your Windows.old folder on your hard drive.
5. More Options: If you click the More Options tab, you'll see this window, taking you straight to the Add/Remove Programs area of Control Panel. It also gives you the option to remove old restore points that take up

space inside Windows. The latest restore point will always be kept in case of a problem with your PC.

6. Programs and Features: This area of Control Panel is one of the most used, although it's not designed to be utilised quite as much in Windows 10 – the idea is that you'd uninstall using the method in the final step on this page. Still, it's the only way to see how much space your desktop applications are taking up. You can also access it via Control Panel > Programs.

7. Other Users: If you try and uninstall a program with other users logged onto the PC, you'll always get a warning that other people may be using the application and so it may not uninstall properly. Get other users to log off before uninstalling programs if this is an issue.

8. Uninstaller: Each desktop app has a different type of installer (or, in this case, uninstaller). Many are very similar, but you do get ones that differ, and one such is this app from Microsoft. Often you will be asked if you want to repair the application. You don't – you want to uninstall.

9. Windows Features: This is for advanced users only. Also from this screen you can select Turn Windows Features On or Off. You're able to uninstall elements of Windows that you don't use – perhaps the old Internet Explorer, for example, or Microsoft's Print to PDF plug-in if you have an alternative solution that you use.

10. Uninstall from Start: You're also able to easily uninstall apps from the Start menu – simply right-click on the app in question and select Uninstall from the menu that appears. It's the best way to uninstall any app, whether it's come from the Windows Store or not.

Storage: How to Move Apps to Different Drives

Windows 10 makes it easier to control where your downloaded apps are installed. There is now no reason to worry about moving your apps to another internal drive. Just a few clicks of your mouse lets you move apps around to whichever storage area suits.

Change Where Apps are Installed

Not every user realises that apps can be installed on the hard drive of their choice, not just the one preselected by the Windows 10 OS. Knowing this is useful for general Windows 10 maintenance.

1. By default, apps you install will be saved to the main partition of the hard drive (usually the C drive). However, you can choose to save them to any other connected drive, both internal and even removable external hard drives (including USB flash drives).
2. In the newer versions of Windows 10, this is a reasonably easy thing to do. Open the main Settings and click on System. Here you will see a whole list of useful sections, but the one you need to open is the Storage section. This will show a visual representation of your storage drives as a whole.
3. Click on 'Change where new content is saved' and a new list will open. Here you can see exactly where apps, documents, music, photos, videos and more are saved by default (unless this has been changed previously). Each of the listed items will have a drop-down menu below it.
4. Click the drop-down menu below Apps and choose the new drive or partition you want apps to be saved to. This only changes where apps (from the Store) installed after this moment are installed. Previously installed apps will still be saved on to the drive that was set when they were added.

Move Installed Apps

If you have a lot of apps installed, moving them to a dif erent drive can be one of the easiest ways to free up space on your main storage volume. Be aware that not all apps can be moved.

1. You can move already installed apps, if you like. There's no limit to the number of different drives you can store apps on. This allows you to make the most of the storage space you have available. To do this, head to Settings > Apps > Apps & features. Click an app and click the Move button.
2. You will then be shown where the app is currently installed and will be asked to choose another drive for the app to be saved on to. Drives are listed in a drop-down menu, with their drive letter shown to make picking the right one easier. Click Move again when you are happy with your choice.
3. You may see a Modify button instead of the Move button. This means the app is a traditional desktop app, and you can't move it. If you see a Move button, but it is greyed out, this is a Microsoft system app and also cannot be moved. You can only move apps installed from the Windows Store.
4. If you move or install apps to an external drive, the apps will cease to work if the drive is unplugged. This is why you cannot move Microsoft system apps to a different drive. Apps that you need to have always available should be left in the main system hard drive partition.

Removing Apps and Software

There are two dif erent ways to remove apps and other software from your Windows 10 computer, but both options may not be available in every instance, so it is useful to understand each.

1. Remove in Settings: In Windows 10, the easiest way to remove apps or other software is in Settings. Open settings and select Apps. Select the program and then select Uninstall. Follow the instructions on the screen. Be aware that some apps built into Windows can't be uninstalled.
2. Remove in Control Panel: On the Start menu, enter Control Panel in the search box and select Control Panel from the results.
Select Programs > Programs and Features, and then select the program. To fix the program, select Repair or, if that's not available, Change. To remove the program, select Uninstall.

Performance: Learn How to Speed Up Windows 10

There are many ways to improve the performance of your PC. Some will produce only marginal improvements and some only speed up operations such as web searches but when you're trying to squeeze the most out of your system every little helps.

Performance without Pain

Gaining improvements in performance is pointless if it means you need to spend 3 hours a day running cleaner software or rooting through old files. These tips will improve performance, without the pain.

1. Install the Latest Windows Updates: Microsoft normally releases updates monthly, although important updates will be released as needed. You should check for and install available Windows Updates, which could include: bug fixes, security patches, Windows Defender malware definitions, etc., that could help keep your system stable and improve the performance of Windows.
2. Use the High Performance Power Plan: By default your PC is set to use the Balanced Power option, which will reduce power to non-essential components when not being used. By selecting the High Performance plan your PC will use more power but should run faster all the time. To change the power plan, search for Power Options in the search bar and then click Additional Power Settings > Show Additional Plans.
3. Switch to a Faster DNS Server: If your Internet Service Provider (ISP) doesn't maintain its Domain Name Server (DNS) properly it will slow down your web searches and make connecting to websites slow and unreliable. Slow and poorly maintained DNS servers are one of the main causes of problems connecting to websites. Consider adding or using a fast DNS server like Google Public DNS in your TCP/IP settings.
4. Speed Up Windows Shut Down Time: If you don't mind delving about in the system registry, you can set and adjust the AutoEndTasks, HungAppTimeout, WaitToKillAppTimeout and WaitToKillServiceTimeout values, which control how long Windows waits for hung programs to close, etc. Remember, the registry is very complex and making changes can have a catastrophic effect on your PC.

5. Uninstall Unneeded Programs: If there are apps or games installed on your system that you just don't use anymore, it's a good idea to uninstall them. This is particularly true of off the shelf PCs that often come preinstalled with a lot of useless software. Fortunately Windows 10 makes this easy, since you can uninstall apps from the Start menu by right-clicking on them and choosing Uninstall from the pop-up menu.

6. Auto Sign in to User Account at Start-up: This is really not recommended for any PC to which others may have access but if you're definitely the only person that will use your PC, you might want to set it so that you don't have to sign in whenever your computer wakes from sleep mode. You can do this in the Accounts > Sign-in options section of the Settings page.

7. Stop the Hard Disk Shutting Down: While having your Hard Disk Drives turn off after a set amount of idle minutes will help save energy, it can also cause your PC to slow down significantly while it waits for the Hard Disk Drive (HDD) to spin back up. Search for Power Options and you can adjust the idle time to never or just increase the amount of minutes. Alternatively you could install a Solid State Drive (SSD), which is always at full readiness.

8. Use the Fast Start-up Option: Windows 10 includes an option to start-up faster by storing an image of the Windows kernel to your hard drive when it shuts down. This saves a lot of time by bypassing a lot of driver loading. In the Power Options, click on 'Choose what power buttons do' and then click 'Change settings that are currently unavailable'. The greyed out settings will become active, including 'Turn on fast start-up'.

9. Enable Write Caching for Your Drives: Speed up the performance of your external storage devices by enabling write caching, temporarily storing data in high speed RAM. Right-click on the Start button and open Device Manager. Expand the Disk drives list and double-click on the drive that you want to enable. Click on the Policies tab and you'll see 'Enable write caching on the device' as a check box option.

10. Keep Your PC Tower Clean: Dust can build up inside your machine forming an insulating layer over vital cooling components and reducing their efficiency, which can have an impact on the performance of your system. It's a good idea to open up the case and give it a good clean once in a while. Obviously disconnect it from the mains first, and use a

soft brush or a compressed air can to blow dust off the CPU cooling fins, etc.

Troubleshooting: Using Windows 10 Troubleshooting Tools

If you have a problem with your Windows 10 machine, you will need to go to the Advanced Start-up Options menu. You may also need to boot into what's called Safe Mode. Hopefully this isn't something you will need regularly but we'll run you through it anyway.

How to Use Advanced Start-up Options

Modern computers are complicated things and there's a lot that can go wrong. If your PC really isn't working correctly or seems slow, these helpful options will help you get it back on track.

1. You may be taken to the Advanced Start-up Options menu. It will appear automatically if you have two consecutive start-up errors on your PC. But you can get to it manually from inside Windows 10 by going to the Settings app > Update & Security, clicking on Recovery and selecting Restart Now underneath Advanced Start-up.
2. If your PC didn't start correctly, you'll see the "Automatic Repair" screen. It gives you the option of restarting and trying again, or clicking on Advanced Options. We're going to run you through what happens if you click on this second button – various options are available to you.
3. You'll then see a menu, which is a little transitional for our liking – we're not sure why these options aren't on the screen you get after this in Step 4 (by clicking Troubleshoot). From here, you can also continue to boot up Windows 10 or you can decide to turn off your PC if you are going to take it to a repair shop, for example.
4. If you selected Troubleshoot, you get the option to Reset this PC. This is a little confusing in name, because it doesn't mean restart! It means resetting Windows to its factory settings (it reinstalls Windows, effectively). You can choose whether or not to keep your files, but we think this is a risky option. You have got your files backed up, haven't you?
5. Advanced Options is actually the menu that we want, and you probably will do, too, if there's something seriously wrong with your PC. It's almost like the previous steps were tests to see if you really did want to

get here. You can try and repair the start-up, or roll back using System Restore.

6. If you select Start-up Settings, you'll be shown this screen to ensure it is actually what you want (you can always go back using the Back button of course). From this you can instigate Safe Mode with or without networking access, as well as a low resolution video mode if you're having display problems.

7. If you have a system image handy (a complete backup of your PC in a system image file) you can also restore it at this point. Anything you've created since the system image was made will be lost, so again it's a reason why you should back up your files.

8. If you need to boot from a particular drive, such as USB, you can do so by starting from it using the boot options in the Advanced Options menu. You can also access the command prompt should you need to do any diagnostic checks of your files, though this isn't a common thing to have to do.

9. When your PC boots after going to Start-up Settings in Step 6, you'll see this menu. You need to press a number to boot your PC in a particular way. We'd always recommend seeing if your PC will boot into Safe Mode with Networking. If it starts up there without issue, it's probably a third-party software or driver problem rather than something with Windows itself.

10. This is what Safe Mode looks like. As you can see, it's very much like the standard version of Windows 10, but it is lacking a little in its graphical finish. It's designed for you to troubleshoot what is wrong with your system – perhaps you need to roll back to an earlier System Restore point, for example.

Troubleshooting: Tips for Diagnosing Windows Problems

Windows 10 includes some useful tools for checking on and solving problems but sometimes you need to look a bit further and deeper. Occasionally you just need to go back to basics. These tips will help you solve some common problems encountered in Windows 10.

First Things to Check

If you're having problems with Windows Update, the Windows Update Troubleshooter might be able to automatically fix the problem. Go to Microsoft.com and search for Update Troubleshooter.

- Windows Update Troubleshooter: Microsoft knows that things don't always go smoothly when updating and have provided a dedicated troubleshooting tool for use during this key task. If you're having problems with Windows Update, the Windows Update Troubleshooter might be able to automatically fix the problem. Go to Microsoft.com and search for Update Troubleshooter.
- Check for Updates: Keeping your copy of Windows 10 up-to-date with the latest releases can really help to avoid problems before they happen. Press the Windows logo key and click Settings. Then choose Update & security > Windows Update and then select Check for updates. Install any available updates and restart your PC if required.
- Checking System Spec: If you're having trouble installing or running a particular app or game, it may be that your PC hardware is not up to scratch. All commercial software will provide details of required and (sometimes) recommended specification needed to run it. You can check system spec at any time, just go to Control Panel and select System and Security, then System.
- App Updates: If an app or program isn't working with Windows 10, particularly after the Anniversary update, try looking in the Windows Store for an update and if that doesn't work, delete and reinstall it. To check for available app updates on the store, click the user icon next to the search bar and select Downloads and Updates.
- Slow Boot Fix: Like Windows 8 before it, Windows 10 uses a hybrid boot to enable fast boot times. It sounds great but can actually slow down

boot for some users. Disable it by searching for Power Options in the Start menu and running the matching Control Panel applet, then in the left-hand pane click Choose what the power buttons do.

- Non-responsive PC: Windows 10 has a completely different shell than previous versions. The Explorer.exe process is still at its core but there are a few additional components as well. If you click the Start button and nothing happens or if the entire taskbar refuses to respond to an interaction, open Task Manager (press Ctrl+Shift+Esc), find Windows Explorer in the task list and click the Restart button.

Fresh Installation Tool

If Windows 10 is really giving you problems and you have tried everything else to fix the issue, you can try using the Fresh Install tool. You will lose any installed apps but will keep your files.

1. First make sure you have the following: an Internet connection to download the tool and the Windows 10 image and sufficient available data storage on the computer you are installing on. You need at least 3GB free for the download and the clean Windows 10 image file.
2. Download the tool https://www.microsoft.com/en-gb/software-download/windows10startfresh. There is some advice on the download page about retrieving and reinstalling Microsoft software such as Office. It is worth checking this out if you are heavily reliant on that software.
3. BACK UP EVERYTHING you want to keep! Launch the tool and review and accept the licence terms. Choose what you want to keep. If you want to keep your personal files, choose the Keep personal files only option. Select the OK button to start the installation.
4. By using the tool, you may lose your digital licences, digital content associated with applications or other digital entitlements. Drivers may also be missing. If you experience any missing drivers after the clean installation has finished, go to Settings > Update & security >Windows Update.

Glossary: Essential Windows Terms

If you have been puzzled by the terminology in this guide, we've added this jargon buster to help; so if you don't know your OneDrive from your Store or your taskbar from your notifications area, then read on.

A Glossary of Commonly Used Windows Terms

Action Center

The new area in Windows 10 that contains all your notifications. It also allows you to access quick functions such as Tablet mode and the Connect menu, which enables you to scan for media devices, such as wireless headphones.

Add-in or Extension

A small application that integrates into another program. Often the context is within web browsers where they add extra functions – such as screenshot sharing or note-taking.

App

Short for "application"; another name for a computer program. An app is a program that has been downloaded and installed on to your computer from the Internet, a CD or DVD or from the Windows Store.

Attachment

A file sent with an email, hence it is 'attached'. The file can then be opened at the other end. It remains self-contained, and is unaffected by the contents of the email itself.

Bluetooth

Bluetooth is a wireless technology used to link and exchange data with another compatible device, and many laptops, tablets and phones have it built-in. Bluetooth devices include headphones, keyboards and speakers.

Broadband

An always-on connection to the Internet via your phone line. If you are served by cable, you can get broadband through this.

Clipboard

The clipboard is an area of your computer's memory that saves items you have previously cut or copied (see Cut and Paste below) ready for you to use them again.

Cloud

The cloud is basically another word for the Internet. It's often referred to in the context of "storing something in the cloud" – this essentially means storing your data on servers that are connected to the Internet. Cloud-based storage (or cloud storage) services include Dropbox and Microsoft's own OneDrive.

Cookie

A small data file that's stored on your computer by websites you visit. Next time you visit the website, the cookie means the site can 'remember' who you are. This is useful for shopping sites, such as Amazon, as they can remember which items you had in your shopping basket.

Cut and Paste

You can move something in a document such as a Microsoft Word file by 'cutting' it, then pasting it elsewhere. The common shortcuts for this are Ctrl-X to cut and Ctrl-V to paste (you can also copy using Ctrl-C). You can also do this to complete files using the same shortcuts.

Desktop

The Windows 10 screen that everything takes place within. The taskbar is at the bottom of the desktop, with the Start button on the left. The desktop is also a place you can store files, in the large area above the taskbar. You can also have a desktop background.

Desktop App

The name for 'traditional' apps in Windows 10. These are applications that you downloaded from the Internet or installed another way rather than obtained from the Windows Store.

Download

When you copy a file from the Internet, it's called 'downloading'. You will have had to have requested the download, for example when you click a document to save it to your own computer.

Driver

A small piece of software that makes a piece of hardware work. Windows 10 includes a lot of drivers as standard (and can download others from the Internet) so common items of hardware, such as digital cameras or phones, can simply be plugged directly in.

Email

Messages sent between computers over the Internet. Mostly they will be text, but can also include attachments. Email is the app that receives and sends these messages in Windows 10 via your email account.

File Explorer

Known as Windows Explorer in earlier versions of Windows, it's the window where you browse through your files and folders. You can also copy, delete, move and create files here.

Folder

A folder icon can store documents, applications, files or even folders and they're stored on your hard drive. Your Documents folder is your default save location in Windows 10.

Gestures

These are finger movements that are used to interact with touchscreen devices, whether it is a phone, tablet or touchscreen laptop.

Icon

A small graphic that represents an application, file or folder on your computer. It can also represent an action within an application, such as Save.

Live Tiles

The large app icons that are 'pinned' to the Start menu. You can remove, resize or add to these. They are 'live' because they continually update with new information.

Microsoft Account

The email address and password you registered with Microsoft. It's needed to buy new applications and entertainment from the Windows Store and is also used by Xbox and Outlook.com and Skype plus other Microsoft services.

Microsoft Edge

The new web browser within Windows 10 that replaces Internet Explorer. It's an app that enables you to view web pages.

Network

A link between two or more computers meaning they can share resources and files. It is also referred to as an LAN (Local Area Network). Most home networks today are wireless (Wi-Fi) networks.

Notifications

Small messages that apps send you to let you know that something has happened – such as an email arriving or that an update is available to download.

Notifications Area

Called the system tray in much older versions of Windows, it's the area of the taskbar to the left of the clock where some utility apps reside (such as OneDrive), as well as key system functions such as Wi-Fi, the battery icon, sound and the Action Center.

OneDrive

Microsoft's own cloud storage service that can be accessed from any device. If you have a Microsoft account, you get OneDrive for free. See 'Cloud' on the previous page.

Peripheral

Any device that is connected to your computer, such as a printer or digital camera.

Search Engine

A website, such as google.co.uk or Bing. com, which enables you to find sites and specific information on the web by entering search terms or keywords related to the subject you wish to find out more about.

Shortcut

A File Explorer icon that points towards an application, file or folder elsewhere on your computer, the idea being that you have easy access to something. All the icons on the Start menu are, in fact, shortcuts to the various operations elsewhere on your computer.

Spyware

Malicious software that seeks to gain information about you without your knowledge. Security applications such as Windows Defender hunt down and remove spyware.

Start Menu

The main graphical interface element within Windows 10 – you get to it by clicking the Start button in the bottom left corner of the Windows desktop, at the left end of the taskbar. From here you can access all the apps on your PC as well as your files, folders and settings.

Tablet Mode

A new mode within Windows 10 that converts the desktop for easier use with touchscreen rather than a keyboard and mouse.

Taskbar

The bar along the bottom of the Windows desktop. It's where all the key functions are and where you can view all your open apps and open the Start menu too.

Toolbar

A block of icons or buttons that carry out certain functions within an application, such as Save or Zoom. In an application such as Microsoft Word, the toolbar is located along the top of the window.

Universal App

A new type of Windows app from the Windows Store. These apps can run on all new Windows devices including Windows 10 mobile phones and the Xbox One.

URL

Standing for Uniform Resource Locator, URL is an Internet address including the 'http://' part. A web address is often referred to as a URL.

Virus

A small program or piece of computer code that ends up on your system without your knowledge. Viruses are created by those with malicious intent and can cause problems with your system. Windows Defender protects you against such threats.

VPN

A VPN (or Virtual Private Network) provides secure access over the Internet to private networks, such as the network at your company or school.

Window

The standard term used to describe an area of screen space used to run an application. You can work within this space. Characterised by a title at the top and buttons to close and re-size the window.

What is Wi-Fi?

Wi-Fi enables devices to connect wirelessly, and if you have a wireless router at home with broadband, you have Wi-Fi. It's also available in many public places such as coffee shops.

Wizard

A utility that takes you gradually through a complex task on your computer. Each screen displays a different step in order to guide you through a particular process, such as installing an application.

Windows Store

The Windows Store is where you can download free and paid-for programs as well as music and video (rented or bought) using your Microsoft account (you need to specify a credit card for paid apps). Access it through the Store icon on the Windows 10 taskbar.

Printed in Great Britain
by Amazon